USN CRUISER
VS
IJN CRUISER
Guadalcanal 1942

MARK STILLE

First published in Great Britain in 2009 by Osprey Publishing,
PO Box 883, Oxford, OX1 9PL, UK
PO Box 3985, New York, NY 10185-3985, USA
Email: info@ospreypublishing.com

Osprey Publishing, part of Bloomsbury Publishing Plc.

Transferred to digital print on demand 2015

First published 2009
5th impression 2013

Printed and bound by Cadmus Communications, USA

A CIP catalogue record for this book is available from the British Library

ISBN: 978 1 84603 466 4
PDF ISBN: 978 1 84908 117 7
ePub ISBN: 978 1 78096 359 4

Page layout by Ken Vail Graphic Design, Cambridge, UK
Index by Fineline Editorial Services
Typeset in ITC Conduit and Adobe Garamond
Maps by Bounford.com
Originated by PDQ Digital Media Solutions, Suffolk, UK

Artist's note

Readers may care to note that the original paintings from which the color plates in this
book were prepared are available for private sale. All reproduction copyright whatsoever is
retained by the Publishers. All inquiries should be addressed to:

The Publishers regret that they can enter into no correspondence upon this matter.

Acknowledgements

The author is indebted to the staffs of the US Naval Historical Center Photographic Section
and the Yamato Museum (formerly the Kure Maritime Museum) for their assistance in
procuring the photographs used in this title.

The Woodland Trust

Osprey Publishing is supporting the Woodland Trust, the UK's leading woodland
conservation charity, by funding the dedication of trees.

www.ospreypublishing.com

CONTENTS

INTRODUCTION

On August 7, 1942 the course of the Pacific War between the United States and Japan, now eight months old, took a new turn. On this date the US Navy mounted its first offensive of the war, landing on the island of Guadalcanal in the Solomon Islands. This first tentative attack prompted a fierce struggle between the US and Imperial Japanese navies, which was to last from August 1942 until February 1943 when the Japanese were finally forced to withdraw from the island. During this time, the two navies fought a total of seven major battles. Two of these, Eastern Solomons and Santa Cruz, were battles between carrier forces. The remaining five were fought between the surface forces of the two navies.

Before the war, both sides expected the question of naval supremacy in the Pacific to be decided by a decisive clash of battleships somewhere in the western Pacific. But the advent of air power and the unexpected scope of Japanese expansion during the initial stages of the war changed that. The US battle line had been crippled at Pearl Harbor and the Imperial Navy preferred to keep the majority of its battleships in home waters in expectation of the decisive battle. When the focus of Pacific naval combat shifted to the south Pacific, following the US landing at Guadalcanal, the bulk of each navy's surface power resided in its cruiser forces. Both sides retained powerful carrier forces after the Battle of Midway, but the limited number of carriers and their demonstrated fragility meant that they were committed only for major operations. With battleships too valuable and potentially vulnerable to be exposed in the confined waters around Guadalcanal, especially at night, this left the cruiser as the major combatant surface ship during the initial parts of the Guadalcanal campaign.

In August 1942 both sides possessed large cruiser forces. In heavy cruisers the Imperial Navy held a numerical, and arguably a qualitative, advantage. Beginning in

1926, the Japanese had added 18 heavy cruisers to their fleet. One of these had been sunk in June 1942 and another so heavily damaged it would not return to service until 1943. The remaining 16 ships were an instrumental part of Japanese naval doctrine and were expected to play key roles in any clash with the Americans. By contrast, Japanese light cruisers were designed to operate in conjunction with the Imperial Navy's destroyer flotillas and were not capable of acting as part of the battle line – unlike the heavy cruisers.

The US Navy had also invested heavily in its cruiser force before the Pacific War. Before the war, a total of 18 heavy cruisers had been built; however, since the US had commitments in two different oceans, not all of these were available for use in the Pacific. Before August 1942 one of these had already been lost to Japanese action, so coming into the Guadalcanal campaign the US Navy suffered from a numerical disadvantage in heavy cruisers. In part, this was compensated for by a number of light cruisers that were much larger than their Japanese counterparts. Nine large light cruisers were commissioned before the war and most were assigned to the Pacific theater. Added to this, the first of the *Atlanta*-class light cruisers laid down just before the war were coming into service by the time the struggle for Guadalcanal began.

Minneapolis shown in November 1942 after taking two torpedo hits from Japanese destroyers. One hit took off the bow as far back as Turret 1 and the second flooded Number 2 fire room. Despite pre-war doubts about their ability to withstand damage, US Navy Treaty cruisers often displayed an ability to take heavy damage, as shown here. (US Naval Historical Center)

Of the five major surface battles fought during the struggle for Guadalcanal, two were contested by forces led by cruisers, and both of these occurred during the initial part of the campaign. The first was the Battle of Savo Island, fought on August 9 immediately after the American landing. Aside from Pearl Harbor, this was the single most disastrous clash for the US Navy during the war and it clearly showed the Japanese cruiser force at its best. Two months later, by contrast, during the Battle of Cape Esperance, an American cruiser force would out-duel a Japanese cruiser force in another confusing night clash. However, these were the last pure cruiser battles fought during the campaign, as in November 1942 the struggle for Guadalcanal came to a head and in two climactic naval clashes between November 13 and 15, both sides also committed battleships. Later, on November 30, a Japanese destroyer force dealt an embarrassing reverse to an American cruiser force in the Battle of Tassafaronga. Because they involved forces based around cruisers on both sides, the battles of Savo Island and Cape Esperance will be used as models to examine the design strengths and weaknesses as well as the employment doctrines of both Japanese and American cruisers.

The battles around Guadalcanal, while costly for both sides, did not prove in themselves to be decisive for the surface fleets of either side. The US Navy suffered more heavily in these battles, but finally learned the techniques necessary to conduct

Brooklyn pictured after her completion in 1937. The arrangement of her five triple 6-inch gun turrets is evident. (US Naval Historical Center)

successful night combat against the Japanese. The design of US Navy pre-war cruisers proved sound and flexible enough to allow them to perform in a number of roles for the remainder of the war. For the Japanese, the results of the Guadalcanal campaign were particularly dire. Though the vast majority of the Imperial Navy's cruisers survived the Guadalcanal campaign, their employment in the fierce battles off Guadalcanal did not the pay the Japanese the dividends they expected. The attrition begun during the Guadalcanal campaign would continue into 1943 as the battle moved to the central and northern Solomons. As the Japanese became more reluctant to commit ships as large as heavy cruisers to these night actions, the Imperial Navy's destroyers were forced to shoulder the burden, a task that eventually gutted the destroyer force. As air power played an increasingly dominant role throughout the Pacific, never again would surface forces play such an important role as they did during the cruiser duels of 1942.

Furutaka pictured after the completion of her major 1937 modernization. Clearly shown are her three new twin 8-inch gun turrets, the quadruple torpedo mounts and the heavier catapult. (Yamato Museum)

CHRONOLOGY

1922

February   Washington Naval Treaty ratified by major naval powers. Cruiser construction is limited by size to a maximum of 10,000 tons per ship and by weapons size to a maximum of 8-inch guns. However no limit on the number of cruisers is set and a building race quickly ensues.

1926

March   Lead ship in Imperial Navy's *Furutaka* class completed; first Japanese heavy cruiser.

1927

September   Lead ship of Imperial Navy's *Aoba* class completed.

1928

November   *Nachi* completed, first of the four-ship *Myoko* class. First of Imperial Navy's Treaty cruisers.

1929

December   *Salt Lake City* completed; lead ship in US Navy's first Treaty cruiser class.

1930

February   London Naval Conference

convened. The resulting treaty places limits on total American and Japanese cruiser construction and creates two categories of cruisers: Type A (heavy) and Type B (light).

May   Lead ship of US Navy's six-ship *Northampton* class completed.

1932

March   *Atago* completed, first of the four-ship *Takao* class. Most powerful of Imperial Navy's Treaty cruisers.

November   *Indianapolis,* first of the two-ship *Portland* class, completed.

1934

February   Lead ship in seven-ship *New Orleans* class completed.

1935

July   Lead ship of Imperial Navy's *Mogami* class completed as a light cruiser. All four ships of this class converted to heavy cruisers before the war.

1937

September   Lead ship in seven-ship *Brooklyn* class completed, the first large US Navy light cruiser. Two more ships

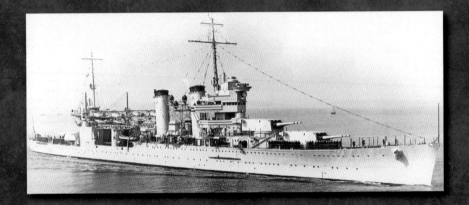

New Orleans was the lead ship of the US Navy's largest class of Treaty heavy cruisers. She presents a much cleaner appearance than preceding classes, and in fact was a better balanced design with greater protection. (US Naval Historical Center)

Atago after completion in 1932. The ship was originally built with 12 torpedo tubes (four triple mounts) and a single catapult. *Atago* also had her bridge modified as *Takao* and was sunk during the Battle of Leyte Gulf in the same submarine attack that damaged *Takao*. (Yamato Museum)

are later completed to a modified design, becoming the *St Louis* class.

1938
November

Lead ship of Imperial Navy's *Tone* class completed as heavy cruisers with significant aviation capabilities.

1939
February

Final pre-war US Navy heavy cruiser completed. Commissioning of *Wichita* brings US Navy heavy cruiser strength up to 18 units.

1941
December 7 Start of Pacific War.
December 24 First ship of *Atlanta*-class light antiaircraft cruisers completed. Eleven ships completed to this design, three after the war.

1942
February 27 Battle of the Java Sea. In the largest naval clash since Jutland in 1916, a Japanese force led by the cruisers *Nachi* and *Haguro* shatters a combined US, British, Dutch, and Australian force.

August 9 Battle of Savo Island. The opening battle of the Guadalcanal campaign results in a smashing defeat for the US Navy. A Japanese force consisting of five heavy cruisers sinks three US Treaty cruisers and an Australian heavy cruiser.

October 11–12 Battle of Cape Esperance. The US Navy turns the table on the Japanese in a confused night action. Four US Navy Treaty cruisers (two heavy and two light) defeat a Japanese cruiser force, sinking the cruiser *Furutaka*.

November 13 First Battle of Guadalcanal. The Japanese commit two battleships to bombard the key American-held airfield on the island but are turned back by a US Navy force led by two heavy and three light cruisers.

November 15 Second Battle of Guadalcanal. Another attempt is made by the Imperial Navy to bombard the airfield with one battleship and two *Takao*-class Treaty cruisers. Two modern US Navy battleships defeat the Japanese attempt, turning the tide of the campaign.

November 30 In the final naval battle of the campaign, a Japanese destroyer force on a transport mission to Guadalcanal defeats an intercepting American cruiser force. The cruiser *Northampton* is sunk and three other cruisers are heavily damaged by torpedoes.

1943
March

Battle of Komandorski Islands. Final cruiser clash of the war. *Salt Lake City* is badly damaged by Japanese heavy cruisers *Maya* and *Nachi* in an indecisive battle.

1945
August

Pacific War ends. Of 18 Imperial Navy heavy cruisers, only two remain afloat, both in a severely damaged condition. Of the 18 US Navy pre-war heavy cruisers, 11 remain.

DESIGN AND DEVELOPMENT

The number and characteristics of US and Japanese cruisers going into the Pacific War were determined by the series of treaties entered into by the major naval powers in the period between the wars. In 1921 the Americans proposed that a conference be convened in Washington with the purpose of limiting future naval construction. What resulted from the Washington Naval Conference was a Treaty for the Limitation of Armament signed on February 6, 1922. The focus of the treaty was on the numbers of battleships that each signatory nation could keep in service or build during the period the treaty was in effect. After existing ships were replaced, both the US and Britain were restricted to 500,000 tons of battleships and the Japanese 300,000 tons. The same tonnage ratio was established for aircraft carriers.

However, because of British objections, no similar restrictions were placed on the construction of cruisers. Nevertheless, all participants did agree that future cruiser construction could not exceed 10,000 tons per ship and that each ship could mount a maximum of 8-inch guns. This limit suited both the Americans and Japanese as it permitted the construction of larger cruisers, better suited for operations in the vast expanses of the Pacific. The unforeseen effect of the conference was to start a race to build more cruisers. With the construction of capital ships (battleships and battlecruisers) mostly eliminated, all major navies embarked on a program of building large cruisers. The treaty placed no limit on the number of these ships that could be built and the 10,000-ton cruiser quickly became the smallest of the future heavy cruiser designs being contemplated by both the Americans and Japanese.

After a failed attempt to place limitations on the overall tonnage of cruiser fleets during the Geneva Naval Conference of 1927, the major naval powers reconvened in

	Type A cruisers	Type B cruisers	Total
US Navy	180,000	143,500	323,500
Imperial Navy	108,400	100,450	208,850

January 1930 in London. By this time the British had relented on their insistence that they be permitted to possess greater cruiser tonnage than the Americans, so for the first time an agreement was reached limiting overall cruiser tonnage. As far as the US and Imperial navies were concerned, the First London Treaty allowed the following tonnage: Type A cruisers were defined as ships with guns greater than 6.1 inches (the 8-inch limit was still in effect), and Type B as those with guns of 6.1 inches or less. For Type A cruisers this constituted a limit of 18 heavy cruisers for the US Navy and 12 for the Imperial Navy. These limits were further defined during the Second London Naval Disarmament Conference held in 1935. By this point Japan had essentially withdrawn from the naval disarmament process, and the conference treaty was signed by the US, Britain, and France. It limited the construction of light cruisers to 8,000 tons, but the US had inserted a provision that this would not pertain to the 10,000-ton *Brooklyn*-class cruisers already under construction.

Japan gave notice in 1936 she would withdraw from naval limitation treaties by the end of 1938. However for some 16 years the naval limitation treaties had defined the size and nature of the US and Japanese cruiser forces, and the resulting ships would form the backbone of their cruiser fleets in the coming war.

US NAVY TREATY CRUISERS

In December 1922 the US Navy building program called for 26 new cruisers – ten *Omaha*-class scout cruisers and 16 of the new 10,000-ton Treaty cruisers. Not until December 18, 1924 did Congress fund the first Treaty cruiser. At this time eight cruisers were authorized, but not fully funded until 1927. These were to become the two *Pensacola*- and the six *Northampton*-class ships.

The US Navy easily accepted the Washington Naval Treaty's 10,000-ton, 8-inch-gun limit for its new cruisers. By 1920 the US Navy had already adopted designs for larger cruisers with 8-inch guns. The General Board, responsible for approving the designs of US Navy ships, foresaw several basic design requirements. As already mentioned, large cruisers would possess better range and seakeeping characteristics essential for Pacific operations. The primary mission of the Treaty cruisers remained scouting. In the era before radar, their range, speed, and comparatively heavy armament (useful for brushing aside enemy screening units) made them excellent scouting platforms. At the same time their heavy armament also made them suitable for missions that the more scarce battleships could not be risked for.

Preliminary designs for the first US Navy Treaty cruiser clearly showed a preference for firepower over protection. The ship was originally designed in 1923 to have 12 8-inch guns, a 35-knot maximum speed and only light protection (0.75 inches of armor over the magazines and 1.25 inches over the conning tower and steering gear). Concern over the lack of protection prompted the General Board to select a design in March 1925 that boasted only ten 8-inch guns and a speed of 32 knots, but which mounted some 1,090 tons of armor.

Design work for the *Northampton* class was already underway before the first ship of the *Pensacola* class had even been laid down. By reducing the number of main guns from ten to nine (mounted in three turrets instead of four), protection could be slightly enhanced and seagoing characteristics improved. Contrary to the expectations of their designers, the first two classes of US Navy Treaty cruisers came in well underweight. The Washington Naval Treaty defined limits in "standard" tonnage. This did not include the fuel and reserve feedwater, but did include stores. This complicated designers' efforts to work up a balanced design within the 10,000-ton limit. In the case of the US Navy, fear of exceeding the limit led to excessive weight-saving measures, as evidenced by the final displacement of the first two cruiser designs. The *Pensacola* actually displaced 9,138 tons and the *Northampton* only 8,997 tons. The nature of these designs gave them excessive metacentric height that resulted in bad rolling in any kind of sea. Due to weight-saving measures, their construction was so light that the firing of all three turrets at once often caused structural damage.

The *Pensacola* and *Northampton* classes were quickly seen as inferior designs, largely for their relative lack of protection. Critics labeled them as "eggshells armed with hammers." As soon as it was realized how much tonnage had been unused in these early designs, the US Navy was determined to do better with a second generation of Treaty cruiser.

After the completion of the first eight Treaty cruisers, in 1929 the US Navy proposed another 15 ships to be built in groups of five. The first group was ordered as an improved version of the *Northampton* class. The principal difference in these ships was a higher standard of armored protection; for example, the side armor protecting the magazines was to be increased from 4.25 inches to 5.75 inches. One ship was to be fitted out as an alternate fleet flagship.

Design work for the second group of five cruisers was also well underway. It was obvious that this was superior to the improved *Northampton* design, so the US Navy decided to retroactively use the superior design on the first group of cruisers. However two ships had already been awarded to private yards and the cost of changing the designs would have been too high. These two ships became the *Portland* class. The other three ships of the first group (*New Orleans, Astoria,* and *Minneapolis*) were built to the improved design, becoming known as the *New Orleans* class.

Completion of the entire second group of five ships was curtailed by the London Naval Conference, and only four were completed – *Tuscaloosa, San Francisco, Quincy,* and *Vincennes.* All these were modified to some extent. Most modifications involved slight redesigns to incorporate weight-saving measures, since after the earlier tendency of American designers to produce underweight designs, they now tended to the other

extreme with the second-generation Treaty cruiser design. None of the *New Orleans*-class ships were designed with torpedo tubes, unlike earlier Treaty cruiser classes. The *New Orleans* class also introduced armored turrets rather than the gunhouses of the earlier ships.

The London Treaty forced a new direction for American cruiser design. The construction of 8-inch cruisers was capped after the completion of the last *New Orleans*-class ship and the final 8-inch cruiser, the unique *Wichita*. The new 6-inch-gun cruisers, known as the *Brooklyn* class, introduced several new features. The aviation support facilities were moved aft, unlike on every other Treaty cruiser class where they were placed amidships. The new 6-inch gun used semifixed ammunition that permitted a high rate of fire. American designers hoped that the volume of fire possible with the 6-inch gun would compensate for the heavier shell used by the 8-inch cruisers. Originally the *Brooklyn* class was to carry 12 6-inch guns in triple turrets, but when the Japanese announced in January 1933 that the new *Mogami*-class light cruisers would carry 15 6.1-inch guns, the early *Brooklyn* design was recast to match the Japanese. The design of these ships was predicated upon providing speed and radius equal to that of the 8-inch-gun cruisers. It was intended that these ships would also possess sufficient armor to withstand 8-inch gunfire. In 1934 the first three 10,000-ton light cruisers were authorized by Congress, after much deliberation on the merits of a smaller design that would permit more ships to be built with the US Navy's remaining cruiser tonnage. In the end it was decided not to accept the firepower and protection limitations of a smaller (8,000-ton) design. Seven ships were eventually built to the *Brooklyn* design.

The last two ships of the *Brooklyn* class were completed to a modified design and became the *St Louis* class. The principal difference was the desire to replace the

A 1940 view of *Quincy* shows the layout of the US Navy's last Treaty heavy cruiser design. As opposed to earlier classes, this *New Orleans*-class cruiser has improved 8-inch turrets, a reworked bridge, pole masts in place of the previous tripod masts and a different placement of the ship's aviation facilities and 5-inch secondary battery. The markings on her turret tops are for aerial identification. (US Naval Historical Center)

5-inch/25 gun with the demonstrably superior 5-inch/38 gun. Instead of the single mounts on the *Brooklyns*, the last two ships featured the first twin dual-purpose 5-inch gun mounts placed on a cruiser. Four were fitted, providing the same secondary armament as the eight single 5-inch mounts found on the *Brooklyns*. The *St Louis* class also featured superior internal arrangements, with the separation of the two engine rooms from the two boiler rooms providing a better ability to withstand battle damage.

The last of the Treaty cruisers was a *Brooklyn*-class ship modified to carry 8-inch guns. The London Naval Treaty of 1930 allowed the US Navy to lay down an 8-inch cruiser in 1934 and 1935. The first ship was the last unit of the *New Orleans* class, but the last heavy cruiser laid down was a hybrid. By using the hull of the *Brooklyns*, steaming radius would be increased and the superior arrangement for the aviation facilities and secondary armament could be adopted. *Wichita* became the design departure point for the very successful *Baltimore* class of war-built heavy cruisers.

US NAVY CRUISER DOCTRINE

Between the wars, the US Navy worked intensively to develop a doctrine that combined aggression with effective control and coordination of all types of fleet weapons to quickly overwhelm and defeat an enemy. The view commonly held by the Navy's leadership was that the coming war would be against Japan and that a decisive battle with the Japanese fleet would be fought somewhere in the western Pacific. This was driven by the US Navy's adherence to the Mahanian view of decisive victory.

In this great set-piece naval engagement, the cruiser force had important roles to play. Cruisers were charged with screening more vulnerable units of the American fleet as the two navies advanced into action. More importantly, cruisers were ideal platforms for performing the scouting mission. They possessed sufficient endurance to operate independently and had the firepower to brush aside enemy screening units to determine the enemy's strength and movement. During the decisive action, most cruisers would operate in the vanguard of the fleet. Destroyers would be used aggressively to attack the enemy fleet, and cruisers would provide fire support to clear a path for the destroyers, but they would keep their distance from enemy units to avoid torpedo attack. During the inevitable exchange of gunfire between the two main fleets, cruisers would also engage enemy battleships and battlecruisers.

While these efforts may have been useful in a major fleet engagement that never happened, they proved utterly inadequate at Guadalcanal. The focus on so-called "major tactics" at the expense of "minor tactics" (engagements between single ships or small groups of ships) would prove very costly.

Night warfare was not ignored by the US Navy, but it was not seen as the decisive phase of combat. Going into the Pacific War, the US Navy assumed that night combat would be decided by the swift application of accurate gunfire. Torpedo tactics were stressed, but were not applicable to the situation that emerged at Guadalcanal. Every exercise stressed the importance of quickly finding the range, and fire-control

procedures had been streamlined in the interwar period. During night combat it would be even more critical to score hits quickly as actions would be fought at shorter ranges. To achieve this, the US Navy developed the tactic of opening fire quickly, even before adequate illumination, and then using the splashes of the shells to determine range. Once the range had been established, a tactic of "rocking" salvos back and forth over the target addressed the unsolvable problem of ascertaining how many shells were actually hitting a target at night. For highly trained crews, this proved an effective tactic. Cruisers of the *Brooklyn* class, with their faster-firing 6-inch guns, were able to smother a target using this tactic. With the advent of radar with sufficient accuracy to allow for radar-guided gunnery, the range was found even earlier and gunfire was more deadly.

Four units of the Pacific Fleet's Scouting Force shown in 1933 maneuvering together to land floatplanes. Scouting was viewed as a primary heavy cruiser mission during a major engagement with the Japanese fleet. (US Naval Historical Center)

IMPERIAL NAVY TREATY CRUISERS

The design of the first Japanese heavy cruisers actually pre-dated the Washington Naval Treaty. However, they were destined to play prominent roles in the Pacific War and influenced subsequent classes of Japanese cruisers. Their genesis was a desire to produce a ship superior to the US Navy's *Omaha* class and the Royal Navy's *Hawkins* class. To do this, the Japanese settled on a 7,500-ton design with six 7.9-inch/50 guns and a 35-knot speed. Because these ships were under the 10,000-ton Washington Naval Treaty limit, their design was not affected when the treaty was signed in February 1922.

The Imperial Navy actually completed four heavy cruisers to pre-Treaty designs. These included two ships of the *Furutaka* class and two *Aoba*-class units. *Furutaka* set the tone for future Japanese cruiser construction, with the design featuring a heavy armament on a fairly small hull and, importantly, the provision of a large torpedo battery. Protection was clearly secondary to firepower. Speed was also emphasized.

Kako shown shortly after her completion in 1926. The ship is in her original configuration with single 7.9-inch gunhouses and fixed torpedo tubes. The three sets of fixed starboard torpedo tubes can be made out just forward of the bridge and aft of the second stack. (Yamato Museum)

As soon as the Washington Naval Treaty had been signed, the Imperial Navy began design work on its first true class of Treaty cruisers. Like the US Navy, the Japanese quickly decided that it made no sense not to build to the full 10,000-ton limit and give the ship 8-inch guns. The original design specifications of the class called for eight 8-inch guns fitted in four turrets (three forward and one aft), four 4.7-inch guns, and eight 610mm torpedoes fitted in four twin mountings. Speed was to be 35.5 knots and range was 10,000nm at 13.5 knots. Armor was not neglected and was to provide protection from indirect fire from 8-inch guns and for critical areas from direct 6-inch fire. As the design was approved in August 1923, it included an increase to ten 8-inch guns, deletion of the torpedo tubes, and a reduced cruising range. Of note, the approved design met the 10,000 limit of the Washington Naval Treaty.

However, as built, the Imperial Navy's *Myoko* class of Treaty cruiser was different. The Navy General Staff was persuaded to bring back torpedo tubes on the ship and change the twin tubes to triple tubes. Another addition brought the number of 4.7-inch guns up to six. These changes and others would clearly bring the ship to over 10,000 tons; when the first ship ran trials, its standard displacement was 11,250 tons. This violation of the Treaty limits was willful on the part of the Japanese and was, of course, not reported.

To keep pace with the US Navy, four additional heavy cruisers were approved under the 1927 Reinforcement Program. This was to become the *Takao* class and would be the Imperial Navy's most powerful class of Treaty heavy cruisers. Originally these were to be follow-on *Myoko* units, but the Imperial Navy decided it could improve the design. Principal improvements included increasing the elevation of the 8-inch battery to over 70 degrees to allow their use in an antiaircraft role. This would permit the number of 4.7-inch guns to be reduced to four. Armor protection was also increased,

particularly around the magazines. Other improvements included fitting two catapults and the exchange of the fixed torpedo mounts for trainable triple mounts. These were mounted on outboard sponsons with the idea that if they ever exploded, the loss of the entire ship could be prevented.

The *Takao*-class cruisers shared a similar hull line with their predecessors, but their appearance was dramatically altered with the inclusion of a large forward superstructure. This large bridge structure reflected the requirement that *Takao*-class ships be fitted as flagships; their superstructures had three times the internal volume of those of the *Myoko* class. They also increased speculation that the Japanese were exceeding cruiser Treaty

Myoko in the configuration in which she would go to war. Her main battery is now 8-inch guns and the 4.7-inch guns have been replaced by twin 5-inch guns. Aft of the second stack, she has been fitted with a raised flight deck with two catapults. The heavy torpedo battery of four quadruple mounts is fitted under the flight deck. (Yamato Museum)

A fine study of *Ashigara* following her 1935 modernization. Note the position of the two quadruple torpedo tubes in their port-side sponsons. This placement was an attempt to mitigate damage if the torpedoes exploded. (Yamato Museum)

limitations. The Japanese were aware that the improvements on the class would add more weight and to compensate they made extensive use of welding – rather than riveting – during construction. Nevertheless the ships exceeded their design displacement by over 10 percent, for a total of 11,350 tons. Ever since the *Furutaka* class, the Imperial Navy had consistently used incorrect design calculations. This practice, never corrected, constituted willful evasion of Treaty limitations.

The completion of the four *Takao*-class units gave the Imperial Navy 12 heavy cruisers – their limit under the London Naval Treaty. Under the treaty, the Japanese still possessed a small amount of tonnage for Type B cruisers. This was combined with a treaty provision that aged ships could be replaced to free up tonnage for a new class of four light cruisers that was to be begun in 1931 and completed by 1937. Work on the new design began in 1930 and, as usual, Japanese designers were tasked with an impossible set of design requirements to be met within a set tonnage limit. The ships were limited to 8,500 tons but were to be armored as well as a heavy cruiser, and still mount a heavy armament of 15 6.1-inch guns and 12 24-inch torpedo tubes. One of the design principles for this class was that the 6-inch battery would be replaced by 8-inch guns as soon as conditions permitted.

To do this, every possible measure to reduce weight was incorporated into the design. In spite of this, design displacement in 1931 was 9,500 tons and stability was

Takao following her completion in 1932. The similarity to the *Myoko* class in overall layout and hull design is obvious, with the salient exception of the massive bridge structure. (Yamato Museum)

dangerously compromised. Concerns about the stability of the design were increased when in March 1934 a torpedo boat capsized in heavy seas and again a year later, when several ships were damaged in a typhoon. In response to the 1934 incident, the design had already been modified for the first two ships, but this did little to ease the stability problems. After the typhoon incident, the entire class was returned to the shipyards for major reconstruction. By January 1938, work on all four ships was completed. This was followed by a 1939 refit for the entire class, which replaced the triple 6.1-inch turrets with twin 8-inch turrets. What finally emerged by the start of the Pacific War was a ship with capabilities similar to the previous classes of heavy cruisers. The *Mogami* class now carried ten 8-inch guns, a secondary battery of eight 5-inch guns mounted in twin gun mounts, and a heavy torpedo armament with reloads. Protection was on the same scale as previous classes of Imperial Navy heavy cruisers.

The final class of Japanese heavy cruisers was laid down in 1934 and completed in 1938–9. This was the two-ship *Tone* class, which was originally to be similar to the *Mogami* class. However, with the mounting problems related to the *Mogami* design, the *Tone* class was recast on an entirely different basis. As reinvented, the *Tone* class would be designed as a heavy cruiser with extensive aircraft-carrying capabilities. This required the main battery to be situated on the forward part of the ship allowing the aft portion to be devoted entirely to aircraft operations. A heavy torpedo armament was still fitted. During the war these ships operated as part of the Imperial Navy's carrier forces; not until late in the war would these ships operate in a dedicated antisurface role.

Suzuya as originally completed. This view shows the layout of her main battery (still 6-inch guns during this period), which employed a unique superfiring position for Turret 3. The position of the torpedo battery has been moved aft as on the *Myoko* class. (Yamato Museum)

This view of *Chikuma* shows the unique configuration of the *Tone*-class cruisers. All four 8-inch turrets are placed forward with the aft portion of the ship dedicated to the operation of as many as five aircraft. (US Naval Historical Center)

IMPERIAL NAVY CRUISER DOCTRINE

Like the US Navy, the Imperial Navy was convinced that the big guns aboard the battleship would be the final arbiter of naval warfare. However, even given this important similarity, the Japanese had developed a very different scheme for employing their cruiser force.

Unlike the US Navy, Imperial Navy cruiser tactics revolved around the use of the torpedo. After the big battleship gun, the torpedo was the Imperial Navy's weapon of choice. Because a torpedo platform had to approach fairly close to its target to be most effective, torpedoes were seen as most useful in a night engagement. However the Imperial Navy spent considerable resources developing a long-range torpedo that could be used day or night. The solution was an oxygen-propelled torpedo that came into widespread service in 1936. This was the Type 93 torpedo, known eventually to the US Navy as the Long Lance. The first ships to receive these top-secret weapons were the heavy cruisers. Tactics for the new torpedo called for the heavy cruisers to fire them in large numbers at extended ranges – day or night – before the enemy was even aware that he was in danger. With the enemy in confusion following the torpedo damage, destroyers would execute further torpedo attacks at closer ranges. This led to intense Japanese rehearsal of torpedo tactics, including large-scale firings day and

night, and constant attention to reducing torpedo reloading times. Given their torpedo superiority, the Imperial Navy believed it would have the advantage in any cruiser engagements.

Night combat was always a central feature of the Imperial Navy's strategy as well as its war-fighting doctrine. Because of its numerical inferiority to the US Navy, the Imperial Navy viewed night combat as an opportunity to inflict attrition on the US battle line and prepare it for defeat at the hands of its own battle line.

To conduct night combat, the Japanese possessed several important tools. Conventional night-fighting tactics relied on the use of large ship-mounted searchlights to provide illumination of targets. However this also provided the enemy with an aiming point, so star shells and parachute-deployed star shells were also developed. Probably the biggest advantage the Japanese possessed at night were the superior optics that often provided vision out to ranges equal to or superior to early American radar. For night combat, each destroyer flotilla was supported by a division of heavy cruisers, together becoming a "night combat group." The cruisers would employ their torpedoes at maximum range and provide gunfire support, allowing the destroyers to penetrate enemy formations.

The four units of the *Takao* class, all shown here with a number of light cruisers, formed the 4th Cruiser Squadron. These powerful ships were an important part of the Imperial Navy's intricate plans for a decisive naval engagement with the US Navy. (Yamato Museum)

THE STRATEGIC SITUATION

The Pacific War between the United States and Japan began on December 7, 1941 when Japan's powerful carrier fleet launched a bold attack to catch the US Navy in its primary base at Pearl Harbor. This attack was successful in changing the predicted course of the naval war in the Pacific, which was shared by both sides. No longer would the war be decided by a clash of battlefleets somewhere in the western Pacific. Air power was now the dominant factor in the Pacific, and naval air power would be the cutting edge of both the US and Imperial navies.

Seizing upon the advantage offered by the crippling of the US Pacific Fleet in Pearl Harbor, the Japanese quickly moved to attain their objectives. After sinking two British capital ships sent to the Pacific to operate from Singapore, the Imperial Navy succeeded in brushing aside weak Allied naval opposition around the Dutch East Indies. The Battle of the Java Sea on February 27 marked the end of any coherent Allied naval defense of the East Indies. It also provided an insight into the strength of the Imperial Navy's cruiser force. To cover their invasion of Java, the Japanese employed a screening force of two heavy cruisers (*Nachi* and *Haguro*), two light cruisers, and 14 destroyers. The Allies assembled a mixed force of American, British, Australian, and Dutch ships, which on paper looked to be an even match for the Japanese. This force included two heavy cruisers (the American *Houston* and another Treaty heavy cruiser, the British *Exeter*), another three light cruisers, and nine destroyers. The battle began with an exchange of 8-inch gunfire at long range. This was inconclusive, and was followed by a barrage of 39 Type 93 torpedoes from *Haguro*, the two light cruisers, and six destroyers. The results were disappointing for the Japanese, with only a single Dutch

destroyer hit and sunk; however this hit and an 8-inch shell hit on *Exeter*, which reduced her speed, threw the Allied force into confusion.

In the second phase of the battle, another mass Japanese torpedo attack of 98 torpedoes, including 16 from the heavy cruisers, rendered no results. In addition, 302 Japanese 8-inch shells also failed to score. The third phase of battle was conducted at night. Four remaining Allied cruisers without destroyer escort again attempted to attack the Japanese invasion convoy. Lookouts aboard *Nachi* spotted the Allied force at 16,000 yards and within minutes another exchange of gunfire ensued, followed by another 12 torpedoes from *Nachi* and *Haguro*. Each of the two Dutch light cruisers was struck by a single torpedo and sank quickly, effectively bringing the battle to an end. In total, two Allied cruisers and three destroyers were sunk against no losses for the Japanese. Though the battle resulted in a Japanese victory, their performance was not overly impressive. The Japanese had launched 153 torpedoes for only three hits, but these were the decisive hits of the battle. Heavy-cruiser gunfire was even less impressive, with only five hits from the 1,619 8-inch shells expended.

While completing the planned conquest of the East Indies, the Japanese were also successfully seizing First Operational Phase objectives in the South Pacific. The large

A view of the *Northampton*-class cruiser *Houston* taken in April 1935. The ship in the background is a *New Orleans*-class cruiser and the differences between the *Northampton* and *New Orleans* classes are evident. *Houston* became the first US Navy Treaty cruiser lost during the war when she was sunk by a Japanese force including the cruisers *Mogami* and *Mikuma* on March 1, 1942 in the Sunda Strait. (US Naval Historical Center)

harbor at Rabaul, located on New Britain, was captured on January 23, 1942. To defend Rabaul, the Japanese considered also capturing other points on New Britain, Tulagi in the Solomons, and key areas on Eastern New Guinea to establish an interconnecting web of airfields with which to fend off potential Allied attacks. On January 29, the Naval General Staff approved the first phase of these operations. Lae and Salamaua, located on southeastern New Guinea, were taken on March 8.

Admiral Ernest King, the moving force behind overall US Navy strategy, was very concerned about the growing Japanese menace in the south Pacific and the possibility that the Japanese would succeed in cutting the sea lines of communications between the US and Australia. King was determined not only to secure these critical maritime links, but also to launch an offensive in the region at the earliest opportunity. Following the Japanese seizure of Lae and Salamaua, the US Navy intervened with a two-carrier strike on the Japanese invasion force. Damage to the Japanese was slight, but it gave them reason to pause before pushing on to Port Moresby and Tulagi. In early April, it was decided to detach two of the fleet carriers from the Imperial Navy's carrier striking force to support future operations in the south Pacific. The next phase of Japanese operations began successfully with the seizure of Tulagi on May 3. The counterattack by an American carrier force led to a clash with the Japanese carriers covering the operation. This action, the Battle of Coral Sea, resulted in heavy carrier losses for both sides but stopped further Japanese expansion in the south Pacific.

Chokai pictured in Truk during the war with a *Yamato*-class battleship in the background. Because of her duties as a flagship, she never returned to Japan to undergo extensive modernization and she remained the least modified *Takao*-class unit. When she was sunk in October 1944 by air attack during the Battle of Leyte Gulf, she still retained her single 4.7-inch guns and triple torpedo mounts. (Yamato Museum)

Myoko as completed in 1929. In her early configuration, she possessed a main battery of 7.9-inch guns and a secondary battery of six 4.7-inch guns. The fixed torpedo battery of six tubes on each beam can be made out just under the single catapult. (Yamato Museum)

Following the clash at Coral Sea, both sides turned their attention to the central Pacific. In a bid for a decisive battle to destroy the US Pacific Fleet, the Japanese launched an attempted invasion of Midway Atoll, but were themselves ambushed with the loss of four carriers. However, even following the disaster at Midway, the Imperial Navy retained an edge overall in the naval balance. In the Pacific, the US Navy deployed four fleet carriers, seven battleships, 14 heavy cruisers, 13 light cruisers, and 80 destroyers. The Imperial Navy still retained four heavy carriers, three light carriers, 12 battleships, 17 heavy cruisers, 20 light cruisers, and 106 destroyers.

Following the Midway interlude, both sides turned their attentions to the south Pacific. On June 13, the Japanese decided to place an airbase on Guadalcanal, the large island directly across from Tulagi where the Japanese had already established a seaplane base. On July 6, two construction units arrived in Guadalcanal to begin work on an airfield.

By the time this work had begun, the Americans were already taking steps to ensure that it would never be completed – or at least not under Japanese control. On June 24, King directed Admiral Nimitz to recapture Tulagi and neighboring areas. By 5 July, planning was already in progress and Guadalcanal was added as a target. Planning was conducted at a frenetic pace and forces were hurriedly marshaled to execute it. The landing would be conducted by the hastily assembled and untested 1st Marine Division and supported by 82 ships under Vice-Admiral Frank Fletcher. These were divided into the Air Support Force with three of the Pacific Fleet's remaining carriers, and an Amphibious Force to land and support the Marines.

Despite the accelerated and, at times, haphazard preparations, the landings on August 7, 1942 went well. Tulagi was captured after a short, fierce fight. On Guadalcanal, Japanese resistance was light, and by the afternoon of August 8 the airfield had been seized.

The Japanese response to the first American offensive of the war was immediate. On August 7 and 8, aircraft from Rabaul attacked the invasion fleet. Both raids resulted in heavy Japanese losses and failed to disrupt the American landing. However a stronger Japanese reaction was already in motion. By the evening of August 7, Admiral Mikawa had already sortied with all available forces, including five heavy cruisers, to strike the American beachhead.

TECHNICAL SPECIFICATIONS

US NAVY CRUISERS
PENSACOLA CLASS

By the time *Pensacola* was laid down in October 1926, the Washington Naval Treaty was fully in effect. The *Pensacola* class was the first American attempt to produce a cruiser under the 10,000-ton treaty limit that still provided an adequate balance of speed, armor, and firepower. The result was the weakest US cruiser design of the Treaty period.

The strong point of the *Pensacola* design was its heavy firepower. The main armament of ten 8-inch guns was mounted, unusually, in four turrets with a triple turret mounted fore and aft in a superfiring position over a twin 8-inch turret. The secondary armament consisted of a battery of four single 5-inch/25 dual-purpose guns. Two triple banks of torpedo tubes were fitted on the main deck in the area of the second stack. Provisions were made for two catapults and four spotting aircraft, but no hanger was provided. Four turbines generated 107,000 shaft horsepower, which was adequate to meet the 32-knot design specification.

The design's weakness was its minimal armored protection. Once the design was found to be some 900 tons underweight, additional armor was provided in the area of the magazine but, overall, armored protection remained deficient. The main belt was between 2.5 inches and 4 inches thick, with maximum protection being provided to the forward magazines. Horizontal protection was 1–1.5 inches. The main armament was actually mounted in lightly armored gunhouses with 2.5 inches of frontal protection. Barbettes were provided with a mere 0.75 inches of armor and only 1.25 inches protected the conning tower.

By the Guadalcanal campaign, several modifications had been made. The torpedo tubes had been removed and an additional four 5-inch/25 single mounts added before the war. *Pensacola* was one of the first Treaty cruisers to receive radar when a CXAM device was fitted aboard in 1940. After the war began, modifications focused on enhancing the antiaircraft armament with the addition of four 1.1-inch quad mounts and some 20mm single guns.

This picture of *Pensacola* shows several of her distinctive features including two aft 8-inch gunhouses (the only US heavy cruiser class to have two aft turrets), her heavy tripod masts, and the placement of the aircraft facilities between her stacks. (US Naval Historical Center)

The first and last classes of US Navy Treaty cruisers pictured together in 1943. On the left are the two ships of the *Pensacola* class next to the *New Orleans*. With their tripod masts, the *Pensacola*s give the impression of being top-heavy. Also note the difference between the 8-inch gunhouses on the *Pensacola*s compared to the turrets on *New Orleans*. (US Naval Historical Center)

USS *Pensacola* (other ship in class: *Salt Lake City*)
Displacement: 9,097 tons (standard), 11,512 tons (full load)
Dimensions: length 585 ft 8 in (overall); beam 65 ft 3 in; draft 19 ft 6 in
Maximum speed: 32.5 knots; endurance: 10,000 nm at 15 knots
Crew: 631 (peacetime)

NORTHAMPTON CLASS

In the *Northamptons*, the US Navy attempted to address some of the shortcomings evident in the *Pensacola* class, but despite some improvements, this class still possessed significant weaknesses. The main armament was reduced to nine 8-inch guns in three triple turrets. The secondary armament remained an unsatisfactory four 5-inch/25 single mounts, and the two triple torpedo mounts were again fitted. Two catapults were also fitted and space provided for four aircraft, but storage for the spotting aircraft was greatly improved with the provision of a hangar around the aft stack.

The same machinery was fitted, but the eight boilers were placed in four separate rooms instead of two as in the preceding class. Seakeeping was also improved, with the selection of a longer hull and a higher freeboard that included raising the forecastle.

The biggest difference from the *Pensacola* class was in the area of protection. Total weight of armor was increased to 1,057 tons, providing for a main belt of 3 inches, with 3.75 inches along the magazines. Deck protection was 1 inch over the machinery spaces and 2 inches over the magazines. The gunhouses received 2.5 inches in the front and 2 inches on the roof. Armored protection of the barbettes was increased to 1.5 inches and conning tower protection remained at 1.25 inches.

Chicago shown in 1940. This view shows the *Northampton* class to be very similar to the previous *Pensacola* class, with the primary difference being the three 8-inch gunhouses on the *Northampton* class instead of the four on the *Pensacola* class. (US Naval Historical Center)

Modifications before the war included the removal of all torpedo tubes. Exercises between the wars had led the US Navy to the conclusion that torpedo tubes aboard cruisers contributed nothing to their combat value, while the effect of an enemy shell hitting the unprotected torpedoes was feared great enough to cripple or sink the ship.

The original four-gun battery of 5-inch/25 guns was doubled to eight guns, beginning in 1938–9. This was seen as a vital step to defend against destroyer attack and to provide a heavier antiaircraft barrage. Further enhancements to antiaircraft defense included installation of a Mark 19 antiaircraft director and eight .50 caliber machine guns. After the start of the war, the antiaircraft fit was increased by the addition of 1.1-inch quad guns when these were available and a variable number of 20mm guns.

USS *Northampton* (other ships in class: *Chester, Louisville, Chicago, Houston, Augusta*)
Displacement: 9,006 tons (standard), 11,420 tons (full load)
Dimensions: length 600 ft 3 in (overall); beam 66 ft 1 in; draft 19 ft 5 in
Maximum speed: 32.5 knots; endurance: 10,000 nm at 15 knots
Crew: 617 (peacetime)

PORTLAND CLASS

The *Portland* class was an interim design combining aspects of the earlier *Northampton* class and the improved *New Orleans* class. The extent to which the prior classes of Treaty cruisers were underweight was now fully evident. This allowed the fitting of additional armor that eventually totaled 5.75 inches on the main belt in the area

Completed in February 1933, *Portland* is shown here in August 1935. Essentially a repeat of the *Northampton* class, this view does show the reduced masts – an effort to decrease top-weight. (US Naval Historical Center)

of the magazines. The remainder of the belt was 3 inches. Horizontal protection was increased to 2.5 inches, the gunhouses again were fitted with 2.5 inches of frontal protection and the barbettes with 1.5 inches. Machinery, main armament, and aircraft handling facilities were the same as in the *Northampton* class. Both ships had the room to be fitted as fleet flagships. *Indianapolis* served in this capacity for much of the war.

Because the ships were completed with a secondary battery of eight 5-inch/25 guns and no torpedo tubes were fitted, the only wartime modifications before the Guadalcanal campaign were again focused on increasing the antiaircraft battery. When available in early 1942, four 1.1-inch quad mounts and as many as 12 20mm single mounts were fitted.

USS *Portland* (other ship in class: *Indianapolis)*
Displacement: 10,258 tons (standard), 12,775 tons (full load)
Dimensions: length 610 ft (overall); beam 66 ft; draft 21 ft
Maximum speed: 32.5 knots; endurance: 10,000 nm at 15 knots
Crew: 807 (peacetime)

This 1936 view of *Tuscaloosa* (left) and *Chicago* (right) undergoing refit shows several of the key differences between a *New Orleans*- and a *Northampton*-class cruiser. Most obvious are the tripod masts and the older gunhouse aboard *Chicago*. (US Naval Historical Center)

USS *SAN FRANCISCO*

USS *San Francisco* was present at the Battle of Cape Esperance and was one of the ships of the *New Orleans* class. Several ships of this class were also present at Savo Island. The *New Orleans* class represented the best of the US Navy's Treaty cruisers.

USS *San Francisco* (other ships in class: *Astoria, Minneapolis, Tuscaloosa, New Orleans, Quincy,* *Vincennes*)

Displacement: 10,136 tons (standard), 12,493 tons (full load)

Dimensions: length 588 ft (overall); beam 61 ft 9 in, draft 22 ft 9 in

Maximum speed: 32.7 knots; endurance: 10,000 nm at 15 knots

Crew: 868 (peacetime)

NEW ORLEANS CLASS

Between 1931 and 1937 the US Navy completed seven cruisers of the *New Orleans* class. These ships were the most modern American heavy cruisers at the approach of World War II and the ships compared well to the Treaty cruisers built by the other naval powers of the day. The redesign begun with the *Portland* class reached fruition with the *New Orleans*. This class provided a better combination of protection, firepower and speed, with the emphasis turning to protection.

In addition to the extra weight made available with the discovery that previous cruiser designs were underweight, the *New Orleans* class was designed with a shorter hull. This meant that the saving in weight could be used to make the main armor belt thicker. Overall, protection now totaled 15 percent of the design displacement, compared to 5.6 percent on the *Pensacola* and 6 percent on the *Northampton* and *Portland*. It was hoped to make the armor adequate against 8-inch gunfire, but this proved impossible. However the main belt was increased to 4–5.75 inches, and horizontal protection to 2.25 inches in the area of the magazines and 1.125 inches elsewhere.

The main battery remained nine 8-inch guns. However for the first time the turrets were fully armored with 8 inches on the front, 2.25 inches on the roof, and 1.5 inches on the sides. Barbette protection was increased to 5 inches on all ships except *San*

Minneapolis seen conducting gunnery drills in March 1939 as a member of the Pacific Fleet. Her aircraft-handling facilities can be clearly seen – two catapults and a hangar capable of accommodating up to four aircraft. (US Naval Historical Center)

Francisco and *Tuscaloosa*, which carried a lighter main turret, and so had barbette armor increased to 6 inches. Because this increased protection brought the ships very close to their treaty limit, barbette protection for the final two ships, *Quincy* and *Vincennes*, was reduced to 5.5 inches. Therefore three different types of 8-inch turret were fitted to the seven ships of the class.

Secondary armament remained eight 5-inch/25 guns but these were grouped closer together, easing ammunition distribution. No torpedo tubes were fitted. Two catapults and space for four aircraft were provided, all moved farther aft. By April 1942 all ships in the class were fitted with four 1.1-inch quad guns and a number (usually 12) of 20mm single mounts.

BROOKLYN AND *ST LOUIS* CLASSES

Construction of the *Brooklyn* class began in March 1935 after a lengthy design process during which the US Navy pondered what to include in its first 6-inch-gun Treaty cruiser design. It was decided that a speed and radius similar to that of the heavy cruisers was required and that a similar scale of protection was desired. The principal difference from earlier Treaty cruisers was the inclusion of a 6-inch gun battery, dictated by the London Naval Treaty of 1930. When the Imperial Navy revealed that its *Mogami*-class cruisers carried 15 6-inch guns, it was quickly decided that the *Brooklyn*s would carry a similar number. These were arranged in five triple turrets with Turrets 2 and 4 in a superfiring position. Secondary armament was the customary eight single 5-inch/25 dual-purpose guns. However the last two ships carried four twin 5-inch/38 turrets. Because these ships also featured modified internal

A stern view of *Brooklyn* showing the arrangement of her aircraft-handling facilities. The two catapults and crane are visible, but below the main deck is an aircraft hangar capable of handling up to four aircraft. This was a clearly superior arrangement compared to previous amidships facilities and was adopted for all future American light and heavy cruiser designs. (US Naval Historical Center)

US NAVY CRUISER WEAPONS

1. The triple 8-inch/55 gun turret (Mark 14) was mounted on *New Orleans*-class cruisers. The rate of fire for each gun was only three to four rounds per minute, later viewed by the US Navy as inadequate for night engagements. These guns fired a 335lb shell and had a maximum range of 30,050 yards at 41 degrees elevation.

2. The triple 6-inch/47 gun turret (Mark 16) was developed for the *Brooklyn* class. These used semifixed ammunition and a 130lb shell. At 47.5 degrees elevation, the maximum range was 26,118 yards. Rate of fire was up to ten rounds per minute.

3. The 5-inch/25 dual-purpose gun was the standard secondary gun on almost all US Navy pre-war cruisers. In its antisurface role, it fired a 54lb shell out to a maximum range of 14,500 yards.

arrangements that made them more resistant to damage, the *St Louis* and *Helena* are considered as a separate class. Another significant design feature was the movement of the aircraft facilities. Two catapults were fitted aft, and space was provided for four aircraft in a below-deck hangar.

Armor protection was 15 percent of total design displacement with a main belt of up to 5.625 inches. Deck armor was 2 inches and the barbettes were fitted with 6 inches. Each turret was provided with 6.5 inches of frontal armor and 2 inches on their roofs. The conning tower was protected by 5 inches.

USS *Brooklyn* (other ships in class: *Philadelphia, Savannah, Nashville, Phoenix, Boise, Honolulu, St Louis, Helena*)
Displacement: 9,767 tons (standard), 12,207 tons (full load)
Dimensions: length 608ft 4in (overall); beam 61ft 9in; draft 22ft 9in
Maximum speed: 32.5 knots; endurance: 10,000 nm at 15 knots
Crew: 868 (peacetime)

IMPERIAL NAVY CRUISERS
FURUTAKA AND *AOBA* CLASSES

The design of the first Imperial Navy heavy cruisers, *Furutaka* and *Kako*, emphasized firepower. As completed, each carried their main armament of 7.9-inch guns in six centerline single-mount gunhouses. Complementing the main battery was a torpedo battery of 12 24-inch fixed torpedo tubes with another 12 torpedoes carried as reloads. Secondary armament was four single 3.1-inch guns.

The two *Aoba*-class ships (*Aoba* and *Kinugasa*) were completed with several important differences. Three twin 7.9-inch gun turrets replaced the single mounts originally fitted on the *Furutaka*. Four of the new 4.7-inch antiaircraft guns were also fitted. Additionally

Kinugasa as completed in 1927. The gun turrets are 7.9-inch twin mounts and the torpedo armament remains in 12 fixed tubes, with three pairs of two on each beam. Modernization before the war would upgrade her main armament to 8-inch guns, provide two quadruple torpedo mounts, and place a catapult aft. *Kinugasa* was sunk on November 14, 1942 by aircraft from USS *Enterprise*. (Yamato Museum)

a catapult was added, which required a redesign of the superstructure aft of the stacks. The stack height and bridge were also modified.

Armor protection for both classes was limited to a main belt of 3 inches. This was insufficient against 8-inch shells, but adequate to defeat 6-inch gunfire at extended ranges. The armored deck was 1.375 inches. The gunhouses were provided with 1 inch of face armor and 0.75 inches of roof armor. The conning tower was not armored.

Being the oldest of the Imperial Navy's heavy cruisers, both classes were extensively updated before the war. When war commenced, they were essentially identical. *Kako* and *Furutaka* each visited the yards twice for reconstruction work, emerging with three twin 8-inch gun turrets, four 4.7-inch antiaircraft guns, a catapult and hangar to operate two floatplanes, and an enhanced antiaircraft fit of four twin 25mm guns and two twin 13mm guns. Significantly, the fixed torpedo tubes were replaced with two quadruple 24-inch torpedo launchers (one on each beam), each with four reserve torpedoes. The machinery was overhauled and stability increased with the addition of bulges. The two ships of the *Aoba* class received similar modifications before the war, except that the work on their machinery was less extensive.

HIJMS *Furutaka* (other ship in class: *Kako*); HIJMS *Aoba* (other ship in class: *Kinugasa*)
Displacement: 7,100 tons (standard), 9,540 tons (full load), (*Aoba* 9,042 tons full load)
Dimensions: length 607 ft 6 in (overall); beam 54 ft 2 in (*Aoba* 51 ft 11 in); draft 14 ft 9 in (*Aoba* 18 ft 9 in)
Maximum speed: 34.5 knots; endurance: 6,000 nm at 14 knots
Crew: 625 (peacetime)

MYOKO CLASS

The lead ship of the class, *Myoko*, was laid down in October 1924. The first ship to be completed in November 1928 was *Nachi*. All four ships were in service by mid-1929. When completed, they were the largest and most powerful cruisers in the world. As completed, the main armament was ten 7.9-inch guns placed in five twin turrets (three forward and two aft). The secondary armament consisted of six 4.7-inch single guns. As on previous classes, a torpedo battery was included, consisting of 12 24-inch tubes fitted in four groups of three in the area of the aircraft catapult. There were provisions for 24 reserve torpedoes, which was increased to 36 in wartime. One catapult was fitted abaft the second stack and space provided for two aircraft, but no hangar was fitted.

Protection was extensive, with a main belt sufficient in length to cover all machinery and magazine spaces. The armored belt was 4 inches and was inclined at 12 degrees. A 305-foot-long torpedo bulge was also fitted and had a maximum depth of 8 feet. Horizontal protection was 1.375 inches on the main deck over machinery spaces and magazines, and 0.5 to 1 inch on the upper deck. The turrets were more accurately gunhouses, since only 1 inch of splinter protection was provided. Barbettes were given 3 inches of armor.

Between 1934 and 1935, all four ships were modernized. Preceding this work, all had their main battery changed to 8-inch guns. Modernization included replacement of the fixed torpedo tubes with two, and then later four, quadruple mounts. Eight reserve torpedoes were carried. The single 4.7-inch guns were replaced by four twin 5-inch mounts. The aircraft facilities were re-worked and raised a level. Space was sufficient for two catapults and four aircraft, but only three were usually embarked.

This overhead view of *Nachi* shows the configuration of the *Myoko* class after modernization. Clearly seen is the placement of the 5-inch guns and the twin catapults. *Nachi* was sunk by US carrier aircraft in Manila Bay on November 5, 1944. (Yamato Museum)

IMPERIAL NAVY CRUISER WEAPONS

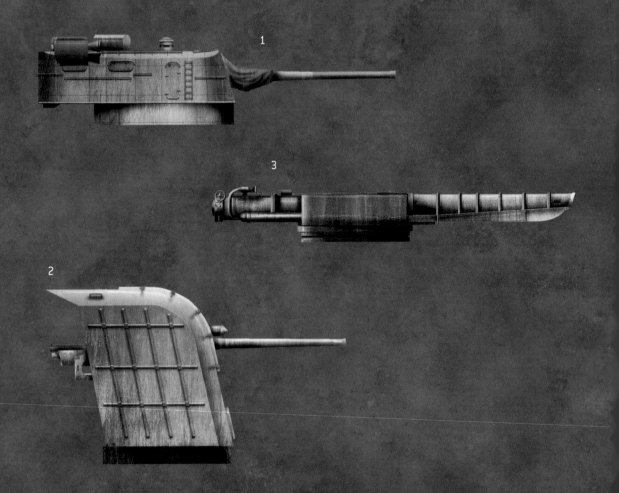

1. The 8-inch/50 Type C Turrets were fitted on ships of the *Furutaka* and *Aoba* classes. This weapon could fire a maximum of four to five rounds per minute (with an effective rate of two to three rounds) and possessed a maximum range of 32,152 yards at 45 degrees elevation.

2. Thirteen of 18 Imperial Navy heavy cruisers were eventually fitted with the 5-inch/40 Type 89 gun capable of engaging surface and air targets. In the antisurface role, it possessed a maximum range of 16,075 yards with a maximum firing rate of 14 rounds per minute (eight sustained).

3. All Japanese cruisers carried a heavy torpedo armament, giving them a firepower edge over their US Navy counterparts. Either a triple mount or a quadruple mount (shown here) was used. The torpedo carried was the 24-inch Type 93 torpedo, know to the Allies as the "Long Lance." These oxygen-propelled, wakeless, high-speed, long-range torpedoes were the most powerful weapons of their kind in the Pacific. The weapon had a large 1,080lb warhead and a phenomenal range of up to 43,700 yards at 36–38 knots.

Bulges were increased to maintain stability. The light antiaircraft armament was increased with the addition of four twin 25mm mounts.

HIJMS *Myoko* (other ships in class: *Nachi, Haguro, Ashigara*)
Displacement: 11,250 tons (standard), 13,300 tons (full load)
Dimensions: length 668 ft 6 in (overall); beam 56 ft 11 in; draft 19 ft 4 in
Maximum speed: 35.5 knots; endurance: 8,000 nm at 14 knots
Crew: 773 (peacetime)

TAKAO CLASS

Construction of these ships began in 1927 and 1928, and they entered service in 1932. In part because they violated Treaty limitations, they were arguably the most balanced and powerful of the Treaty cruisers. As improved versions of the *Myoko* class they shared many characteristics. Main armament was ten 8-inch guns, arranged identically to *Myoko*. However these turrets were designed with a 70-degree elevation (see opposite), permitting them to be used as antiaircraft guns, but this concept proved a failure in service. The secondary battery still employed 4.7-inch guns, but only four were fitted. A heavy torpedo armament remained an important design feature. It was

Ashigara pictured during the early period of the war. The aircraft is an E13A1 Type 0 long-range reconnaissance floatplane (Allied codename "Jake"), the floatplane most used on Japanese heavy cruisers during the war. *Ashigara* spent most of the war assigned to secondary theaters. On June 7, 1945 she was sunk by a British submarine while on a transport mission in the East Indies. (Yamato Museum)

envisioned that four triple mounts could be fitted, but weight considerations reduced this to twin mounts. Sixteen spare torpedoes were carried and the Japanese went to great efforts to devise quick reloading systems.

Protection was increased to a maximum of 5 inches for the main belt, tapered down to 1.5 inches in its lower edges. The main deck was armored with 1.375 inches in the area of the magazines. The upper deck included 0.5 to 1 inch of armor. The conning tower was armored and the turrets were given 1 inch of protection.

Before the war, an attempt was made to modernize the class. *Takao* and *Atago* received the most work and each had their torpedo armament increased to four quadruple mounts with a new quick reload system. New catapults were fitted and six dual 25mm guns were fitted. The appearance of these two ships was altered when the forward superstructure was rebuilt in an effort to save weight. Early in the war *Atago*

and *Takao* exchanged four twin 5-inch gun mounts for their single 4.7-inch mounts. *Chokai* and *Maya* received more limited modernization in early 1941. The ships were modified to fire the Type 93 torpedo, new catapults were fitted, and minimal additions made to their light antiaircraft battery. *Chokai* never received the heavier torpedo armament and 5-inch secondary battery guns before she was sunk, and *Maya* did not receive these upgrades until 1944.

MOGAMI CLASS

To comply with the London Naval Treaty, this four-ship class was designed as a light cruiser with 15 6.1-inch guns and a heavy torpedo armament of 12 24-inch tubes. In addition to this, the magazines were to be protected against 8-inch gunfire and the machinery spaces protected against 6-inch gunfire. As already indicated, this proved impossible on an 8,500-ton hull. After a period of redesign and reconstruction, the *Mogami*s did finally emerge as attractive and powerful ships. After being rearmed, their main battery consisted of ten 8-inch guns arranged in five twin turrets, three forward and two aft. The secondary battery included four twin 5-inch guns. Light antiaircraft weaponry was limited to four twin 25mm mounts. The torpedo battery consisted of 12 24-inch torpedo tubes (four triple mounts) and included 12 reserve torpedoes with provision for quick reload. These were located on the main deck in the area of the aircraft facilities. Two catapults were fitted and there was sufficient space for three aircraft.

Armor compared favorably with previous classes of design-built heavy cruisers. The main belt was 4 inches thick in the area of the machinery spaces and increased to 5.5 inches in the area of the magazines. The upper edges of the belt met the horizontal armor, which varied from 1.375 inches to 2.375 inches. Barbette armor was 3–4 inches.

Maya as seen before the Pacific War, but after her limited modernization. She retains her massive bridge structure, triple torpedo mounts, and 4.7-inch gun mounts. In 1943, after receiving damage from a US carrier-borne air attack, she was modified as an antiaircraft cruiser receiving 12 5-inch guns in six twin mounts. She was sunk by submarine attack during the Battle of Leyte Gulf in October, 1944. (Yamato Museum)

OPPOSITE:
A fine study of the bridge structure of *Chokai*. In addition to the fire control and optical equipment evident, the triple torpedo mount and the single 4.7-inch gun can clearly be seen. (Yamato Museum)

HIJMS *CHOKAI*

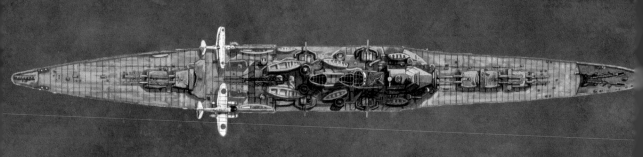

HIJMS *Chokai* in her 1942 configuration. She was the flagship of the Imperial Navy's victorious cruiser force at the Battle of Savo Island and, as a ship of the *Takao* class, represented the epitome of Japanese cruiser design.
HIJMS *Takao* (other ships in class: *Atago, Maya, Chokai*)
Displacement: 11,350 tons (standard), 15,490 tons (full load)

Dimensions: length 668ft 6in (overall); beam 59ft 2in; draft 20ft 1in
Maximum speed: 35.5 knots; endurance: 8,000nm at 14 knots
Crew: 773 (peacetime)

HIJMS *Mogami* (other ships in class: *Mikuma, Suzuya, Kumano*)
Displacement: 8,500 tons (standard, as designed), 11,169 tons (full load)
Dimensions: length 661 ft 1 in (overall); beam 59 ft 1 in; draft 18 ft 1 in
Maximum speed: 37 knots; endurance: 8,150 nm at 14 knots
Crew: 850 (peacetime)

Mogami pictured after January 1938 following the completion of her reconstruction. In this configuration, she retained a main battery of 15 6-inch guns. These were removed and replaced by 8-inch guns before the war. (Yamato Museum)

TONE CLASS

The two ships of the *Tone* class were designed as aircraft-carrying cruisers. The entire battery of eight 8-inch guns was concentrated forward in four twin turrets. Secondary armament consisted of the customary eight 5-inch guns in four twin turrets. Torpedo armament still remained heavy with 12 tubes in four triple mounts, all situated in the area of the catapult. The quarterdeck area was free of armament, so up to five aircraft could be carried. Two catapults were fitted. Protection was similar to the *Mogami* class, but was arranged differently internally.

HIJMS *Tone* (other ship in class: *Chikuma*)
Displacement: 11,215 tons (standard), 15,200 tons (full load)
Dimensions: length 661 ft 1 in (overall); beam 60 ft 8 in; draft 21 ft 3 in
Maximum speed: 35 knots; endurance: 9,000 nm at 18 knots
Crew: 850 (peacetime)

THE COMBATANTS

US NAVY CRUISER CREWS

Life on a warship was a combination of hard work, conformity, and, in wartime, occasional moments of terror and exhilaration. Cruiser crews were fairly small, and sailors were often assigned to the same ship for many years, making the crew a tight-knit organization. Unlike battleships, where spit and polish seemed to be more important at times than the business of practicing to fight, cruisers spent a great deal of time at sea and their capabilities were honed to a fine edge.

The primary purpose of a cruiser was to act as a gun platform. Gunnery thus became the focus of much of the crew's daily activities. A retired naval officer described the routine of a 5-inch/25 gun crew as thus:

> The pointer elevated the gun either by matching signals sent from the director, or by eye. The trainer trained the gun in azimuth by the same method. The fuze setter set a timing mechanism on his "fuze pots," in accordance with the director order, or the order of the gun captain ... A third loader would strip the protecting wires from the rim of the can [containing the shell] and tilt the can so the ammunition could be handled by the second loader. This man than placed the [shell] nose-down in one of the three fuze pots, which set the mechanical/powder fuze. The first loader would reach over, pick up a shell from the fuze pot, and place it on a tray under the chamber of the gun. The gun captain would shove a lever, and the shell would be rammed home by compressed air. Automatically, the breech would close ... the gun would fire, recoil, and eject the empty cartridge. The first loader would start the action all over again by placing another shell on the tray. This was an amazingly fast and efficient method. We could load and fire twenty or more shells a minute over a sustained period. The enlisted men were drilled for interminable hours into teams of near-inhuman perfection.

A cruiser's crew was organized into eight departments, each performing one of the primary functions of the ship. These included gunnery, navigation, communications, engineering, repair, medical, supply, and aviation. Each department could have several different divisions to address each of the specialized duties required of each department. All members of the ship's company were assigned a General Quarters station that was to be occupied during battle. In addition, most crewmen were also assigned watches to be performed in addition to their regular duties. Sleep was a precious commodity, especially during wartime in combat areas when the entire crew could be at General Quarters for extended periods.

Going into the Pacific War, the US Navy possessed a large number of competent officers proficient in both technical and operational matters. Years of training had given them a shared sense of aggression and, as events during the war would demonstrate, the ability to adapt quickly to change. Officers were mostly graduates of the Naval Academy located in Annapolis, Maryland. However during the interwar years there were still officers remaining from the expansion during World War I, and, beginning in 1925, the Navy took officers into service through the Reserve Officer Training Course. Going into the Pacific War, all major commands (like that of the

One of the 5-inch/25 gun crews aboard *Astoria* in early 1942. Note the crew still wearing the vintage World War I-style helmets. The 5-inch gun was a dual-purpose weapon capable of engaging both surface and air targets. (US Naval Historical Center)

REAR ADMIRAL NORMAN SCOTT (1889–1942)

Norman Scott had the fortune of being the first US Navy officer to beat the Japanese in a surface battle during the Pacific War. He won his victory at a time when America was short of naval heroes, thus magnifying his fame and reputation.

He was born in Indianapolis, Indiana and was admitted to the Naval Academy in 1907. After graduation, Ensign Scott served in the battleship *Idaho* and then on destroyers. In December 1917 he was the executive officer of a destroyer that was sunk by German submarine attack; Scott was commended for his performance in the incident. For the remainder of the war he served in the US, including as an aide to President Wilson.

After the war he commanded a division of Eagle Boats, and during the early 1920s Scott returned to destroyers, followed by duty aboard the battleship *New York*. From 1924 to 1930 he was assigned to the staff of Commander, Battle Fleet and served as an instructor at the Naval Academy. In the early 1930s, he commanded two destroyers, followed by a stint at the Navy Department and attendance at the Senior Course at the Naval War College. As a commander, he served as executive officer aboard the cruiser *Cincinnati* and later as a member of the US Naval Mission to Brazil in 1937–39. Following promotion to the rank of captain, he was commanding officer of the heavy cruiser *Pensacola* until shortly after Pearl Harbor.

Captain Scott was assigned to the staff of Admiral King during the first months of 1942. After promotion to rear

Norman Scott, shown here as a captain. (US Naval Historical Center)

admiral in May, he was granted his wish of being posted to a combat command in the Pacific. Scott commanded a surface task group for the first three months of the Guadalcanal campaign, but always seemed to miss out on the action. As Commander Task Group 62.4 (the most eastern group of the transport screen) during the Battle of Savo Island, he saw no action. He commanded the

commanding officer of a cruiser) were held by Annapolis graduates. But not until 1933 was Annapolis accredited as offering an equivalent education to a civilian university. Attendance at the school was an arduous four years that stressed development of leadership skills at the expense of academic training.

When an officer graduated as an ensign, his first tour was spent as a surface warfare officer. It was during this tour that the young officer had to learn every aspect of how to operate and fight his ship. This was a prerequisite to other career alternatives like submarine duty or aviation. Competition remained part of an officer's life and for each rank he had to undergo a selection process. Promotion boards would review his record and decide if he was suitable for promotion. Those judged unfit for promotion were dismissed from the Navy or forced to retire. Especially promising officers would endeavor to attend the Naval War College located in Newport, Rhode Island. In the screen of the carrier *Wasp* at the Battle of the Eastern Solomons, but a poorly timed refueling forced *Wasp* to miss the battle. Finally, on the night of October 11–12, Scott's chance would come. With a force of four cruisers and five destroyers, he entered the waters north of Guadalcanal to contest the Imperial Navy's total control of the night waters around the island. The result was a victory, though inconclusive, for the US Navy. For a loss of a single destroyer, Scott's force sank a heavy cruiser and a destroyer and did much to raise American morale. Scott's performance at the Battle of Cape Esperance was far from perfect, but he made fewer mistakes than his Japanese adversary and he demonstrated that the Imperial Navy could be beaten, even at night. He made every possible effort to prepare his force for action and gave them a clear battle plan. Most of all, he was aggressive, taking the battle to the Japanese in a way that they did not expect.

In November, command of the US Navy's surface task group operating off Guadalcanal was given to Rear Admiral Daniel Callaghan. Despite the fact that Scott had been serving six months at sea and had the success at Cape Esperance behind him, Vice-Admiral Turner chose to give command to the newcomer Callaghan because, most likely, he was 15 days senior to Scott as a rear admiral. Seniority meant everything in the US Navy. As deputy commander to Callaghan during the night action known as the Naval Battle of Guadalcanal on November 13, Rear Admiral Norman Scott was killed in action when his flagship, the light cruiser *Atlanta*, was struck by gunfire and a torpedo. For his actions in the October and November battles, Scott was posthumously awarded the Medal of Honor. The citation of the award read as follows:

For extraordinary heroism and conspicuous intrepidity above and beyond the call of duty during action against enemy Japanese forces off Savo Island on the night of 11–12 October and again on the night of 12–13 November 1942. In the earlier action, intercepting a Japanese Task Force intent upon storming our island positions and landing reinforcements at Guadalcanal, Rear Adm. Scott, with courageous skill and superb coordination of the units under his command, destroyed 8 hostile vessels and put the others to flight. Again challenged, a month later, by the return of a stubborn and persistent foe, he led his force into a desperate battle against tremendous odds, directing close-range operations against the invading enemy until he himself was killed in the furious bombardment by their superior firepower. On each of these occasions his dauntless initiative, inspiring leadership and judicious foresight in a crisis of grave responsibility contributed decisively to the rout of a powerful invasion fleet and to the consequent frustration of a formidable Japanese offensive. He gallantly gave his life in the service of his country.

interwar years, not only was this a center of innovation in the US Navy, but it was a virtual prerequisite for promotion to flag rank. Here students studied tactical and strategic problems, often using war gaming. Cruiser doctrine was largely developed here.

The level of training and education of the US Navy's sailors going into the war was quite high. It is worth noting that conscription into the Navy did not begin until December 1942 – thus all cruiser crews going into the war were composed of volunteers, many of whom had served considerable periods of time on the same ship.

A sailor was drawn into service in the US Navy for many of the same reasons as were his officers. Naval service held the promise of travel and adventure, and, during the Great Depression, guaranteed food, accommodation, and a regular paycheck. During the 1930s many well-educated men (those possessing a high-school degree) were drawn to the Navy as few opportunities existed elsewhere. Upon enlisting, basic

The wardroom of *Augusta* pictured in 1937. Of the crew of more than 600 on a *Northampton*-class cruiser, only some 40 were commissioned officers. (US Naval Historical Center)

training consisted of 12 weeks. At this point the apprentice seaman was sent to his first ship, where he was expected to learn a trade and become rated in a particular skill. Before the war, about half the crew would be comprised of sailors who were "striking" for a rate. Once he had learned a skill, and had demonstrated other traits such as reliability and leadership, he could be advanced to seaman and later petty officer. Long-serving sailors who had demonstrated exceptional technical skills and leadership were selected to be chief petty officers, who were instrumental in the smooth running of the ship. Enlisted personnel were advanced through exams using instruction books published by the Bureau of Navigation.

Conditions aboard ship were hard, but by no means brutal. Enlisted men ate in their own areas, separate from the officers and the chief petty officers who each had their own mess areas. By the late 1930s cafeteria-style berthing had replaced the old-style mess, where sailors would take food from a central galley to their mess area. Berthing areas were always crowded and sailors slept in pipe rack bunks. However, during the war, as crew sizes grew with the addition of more men required to service the growing numbers of antiaircraft guns or electronics, conditions on board cruisers became much more cramped. When added to the rigors of prolonged duty in tropical areas (like Guadalcanal), conditions were barely tolerable.

IMPERIAL NAVY CRUISER CREWS

While American crews practiced seriously for war, the crews of Imperial Navy cruisers took combat training to another level. Part of the Imperial Navy's ethos was that numerical inferiority had to be compensated for with superior personnel training and readiness. This could be accomplished only through constant and rigorous exercising. In the 1920s the Combined Fleet's commander ordered the fleet to engage in night combat exercises "more heroic than under actual battle conditions." The seriousness of his intent was revealed in August 1927 when, during a night torpedo exercise, four ships collided at high speed resulting in the loss of one destroyer with 104 casualties, another destroyer heavily damaged with 29 more casualties, and serious damage to two cruisers. Training was often conducted in northern waters in severe weather and sea conditions, and the pace was relentless; there was no such thing as a weekend in the pre-war Imperial Navy and shore leave was reduced to two or three successive days each month.

The Imperial Navy's training year began on December 1 and focused on single-ship and squadron-level training through April. This progressed into training with the entire Combined Fleet in May, reaching a climax in October. As far as possible,

The chief petty officers of *Tuscaloosa* pictured with President Roosevelt in 1940. Chief petty officers were the most senior enlisted personnel in the crew and were instrumental in maintaining discipline and training new crew members. (US Naval Historical Center)

VICE-ADMIRAL MIKAWA GUN'ICHI (1888–1981)

Mikawa was destined to become one of the Imperial Navy's more controversial command figures of the Pacific War. Born in Hiroshima Prefecture in 1888, he graduated from the Eta Jima in 1910 third in his class of 149. He was identified early on as an officer of great potential, as evidenced by his posting to the Naval Staff College in 1916 and his extensive overseas assignments.

Like most Imperial Navy officers, much of his time was spent at sea. As a midshipman he spent time on four different ships before attending the Naval Torpedo and Gunnery Schools in 1913–14. His first assignment as a young officer was aboard the cruiser *Aso* and he later served aboard a destroyer and a transport during World War I. After attending the Versailles Peace Treaty Conference as a member of the Japanese delegation, Lieutenant Mikawa returned to the fleet, where he held the position of chief navigator aboard several ships including the battleship *Haruna*; for the remainder of his career he was considered a specialist in navigation. His sea tours were followed by a period of duty as an instructor at the Naval Torpedo School, and as a new commander he was part of the Japanese delegation to the London Naval Conference. This was followed by a period as the naval attaché in Paris. Promoted to captain in 1930, he returned to Japan to assume administrative and training duties.

As a captain he served as commanding officer on several ships in the mid-1930s, including the cruisers *Aoba* and *Chokai*, and the battleship *Kirishima*. In December 1936 he gained flag rank.

Vice-Admiral Mikawa Gun'ichi. (US Naval Historical Center)

As a rear admiral he continued to be given important posts as Chief of Staff of the Second Fleet and on the Navy General Staff and at Imperial General Headquarters. This was followed by command of cruiser and battleship squadrons before he was promoted to vice-admiral in November 1940.

When war came he was commander of Battleship Division 3 (the *Kongo*-class units) and, leading the First Section of his squadron, was assigned as the commander

combat conditions were replicated during training. The rigor of these exercises was such that Japanese officers often described it as tougher than actual combat. Added to peacetime exercises was the advantage of exposing ships to actual combat conditions off the Chinese coast after 1937.

All considered, the Imperial Navy entered the Pacific War as an extremely confident and competent force. Training in night combat was particularly well honed. For the first part of the war, the performance of the Imperial Navy's surface combatants confirmed the Navy's faith in its pre-war training. Of Guadalcanal, it is hard not to come to the conclusion that Japanese cruiser crews were better trained than their counterparts in the US Navy. This was only accomplished by the rigorous and incessant pace of peacetime training.

of the screen of the First Air Fleet (the Imperial Navy's carrier force). He continued to command battleships during the Indian Ocean operation in April 1942 and during the Battle of Midway as part of the Midway Occupation Force.

In July 1942, he was given command of the new 8th Fleet, also known as the Outer Seas Force. The lack of concern shown by the Naval General Staff about guarding its new conquest in the south Pacific was shown by the lack of forces assigned to Mikawa. He did have the *Chokai* as his flagship, but the rest of his command included Japan's four oldest heavy cruisers, three old light cruisers, and eight destroyers that were equally outdated.

Mikawa reached Truk on July 25 en route to his new command. In discussion with the staff of the Combined Fleet before arriving in Truk, and after talking to officials there, he quickly discovered that nobody considered the Americans posed a serious threat to the Solomons. On July 30 he arrived at Rabaul to assume his new post; a week later he was in combat facing the first American offensive of the war.

In his first encounter with the US Navy he gave the Americans a severe beating at the Battle of Savo Island. He continued in command of the 8th Fleet throughout the campaign, personally leading the cruiser bombardment of Henderson Field on the night of November 13–14. He was also the primary organizer of the "Tokyo Express" that was the only means of getting troops and supplies to the island in the face of American air superiority. In April 1943 he was relieved as commander of the 8th Fleet.

Following his relief, Mikawa was assigned to duties in Japan. In September 1943 he was given a rear area post as commander of the Second Southern Expeditionary Fleet in the Philippines; he assumed command of the Southwestern Area Fleet in the Philippines from June to October 1944. After the disastrous Battle of Leyte Gulf he was again relieved, and returned to Japan, concluding his active duty service in May 1945. He lived until February 1981.

Mikawa is described as intelligent and soft-spoken. It is also obvious that he was very aggressive, as demonstrated by his audacity during the Guadalcanal campaign. His career had exposed him early and often to the classic precepts of Imperial Navy education, first and foremost that naval power comes from the defeat of the enemy's battle fleet. As discussed later in this book, this may have been the primary factor why he failed to turn his tactical victory at Savo Island into a strategic victory by attacking the American transports off Guadalcanal whatever the cost. This lack of flexibility was also a characteristic of the Imperial Navy's officer corps, even its best officers, as Mikawa clearly was. It is significant that his failure to attack the transports was not seen as a fatal blunder by the Japanese at the time. Mikawa continued to act as 8th Fleet commander and performed well in that capacity. Even after the shake-up following the defeat at Guadalcanal, he continued to hold important commands. On balance, it is fair to say that Mikawa epitomized the best and the worst traits of the Imperial Navy's officer corps.

One of the Imperial Navy's strongest characteristics was the quality of its enlisted crew personnel. In 1942 the Imperial Navy comprised 34,769 officers and 394,599 enlisted members. Prior to the war, the enlisted force was about one-third volunteer and the remainder conscript. Of course, the Japanese preferred the former as they served longer and thus were more likely to fully absorb the increasingly complex business of manning a modern warship. After the war began, this shifted to a 50-50 mix of volunteers and conscripts. Generally the enlisted crew and the officers served well together. However life aboard a Japanese cruiser was not easy. In addition to the high operational tempo even during peacetime, lower-ranking enlisted personnel were often subjected to physical abuse by petty officers or even officers. There were no creature comforts aboard a cruiser, or any other Imperial Navy warship, as habitability was a very low design priority.

Aoba pictured with the carrier *Kaga* in the background. After the modernization of the *Furutaka* class, the principal differences between the *Furutaka* class and the *Aoba* class were the thicker second stacks on the *Aobas* and the different catapult placement, with *Aoba*'s being further aft. (Yamato Museum)

The Imperial Navy's well-trained, disciplined, and motivated enlisted force was combined with an excellent officer corps. Almost all Japanese naval officers entered service through the Naval Academy located on the island of Eta Jima near Hiroshima. Entrance into the academy was extremely competitive. For example, in 1937 more than 7,100 applicants contended for 240 places. Eta Jima stressed fitness and toughness. Life was spartan and new midshipmen were subjected to brutal beatings at the hands of upperclassmen, setting the tone for service in a navy where beatings were all too commonplace. The quality of instruction at Eta Jima was generally good, but newly minted ensigns left the academy with a generally inflexible mindset.

The Imperial Navy's manning strategy was built around creating a small, highly trained cadre of career officers and men. During the initial period of war, this strategy proved successful. However under the strain of war, when the Japanese were attempting to expand the fleet and replace losses, it was clearly insufficient. The high caliber of Japan's cruiser crews, nor of the entire Navy, could not be maintained.

COMBAT

Word of the American landings on Tulagi and Guadalcanal on August 7 quickly reached the headquarters of the Imperial Navy's 8th Fleet in Rabaul. Within hours the fleet commander, Vice-Admiral Mikawa, had decided to attack the American landing force with whatever forces were available. For his attack, Mikawa could gather the following force:

Flagship	Heavy cruiser	*Chokai*
Cruiser Division 6	Heavy cruisers	*Aoba*
		Kinugasa
		Kako
		Furutaka
Cruiser Division 18	Light cruisers	*Tenryu*
		Yubari
Destroyer		*Yunagi*

By 1430 hours, the Japanese had put together a plan, had it approved by Tokyo, and were departing Rabaul. Mikawa was unsure of the enemy's strength, but his extremely aggressive plan was banking on the night-fighting excellence of the Imperial Navy's cruisers. It should be noted though that this scratch force had never exercised or fought together, with the exception of the ships of Cruiser Division 6. Nevertheless, as noted by an 8th Fleet staff officer, morale and expectations were high as the Japanese began the operation:

> It was a fine clear day, the sea like a mirror. Our confidence of success in the coming night
> battle was manifest in the cheerful atmosphere on the bridge [on flagship *Chokai*]

53

Group A (Yubari, Tenryu, Furutaka)
Group B (Chokai, Aoba, Kako, Kinugasa)

Yunagi
Yubari
Tenryu
Furutaka
Kinugasa
Kako
8th Fleet   Aoba
(Vice Admiral   Chokai
Mikawa)   ● 00 54

● 02 50   ● 0240

Ralph
Talbot

Florida Island

02 25   00 20

01 05 ●   02 10 ● 02 25

Northern Group   ● 00 50

● 00 40   02 36   Astoria
Blue   Vincennes   Quincy   Wilson Quincy
          02 50   Quincy   02 11   Vincennes
Yunagi   Savo Island   ●   Helm
          02 15   01 50   ● 01 40
01 20 ●   Astoria   ● 01 55   ● 02 00
                    Group A   Group B
                    ● 01 50

02 36 ●   ● 01 36   Canberra

Cape Esperance   Chicago   ● 01 43
                              Bagley   Southern Force
                    Canberra   Chicago
                    Patterson

GUADALCANAL

Awaiting the Japanese was an Allied force under the command of Rear Admiral Richmond "Kelly" Turner. Turner had been given command of the Amphibious Force; in turn, he appointed British Rear Admiral Victor A. C. Crutchley (who had been seconded to the Royal Australian Navy) as his deputy, despite the protests of the latter that an American should receive the job. Turner's deployment to guard the transports of the invasion fleet was as follows:

This color photo of *Quincy* in 1942 shows the ship in a modified Measure 12 camouflage scheme. *Quincy*'s wartime career was very short, being transferred to the Pacific in June 1942, and sunk shortly thereafter at the Battle of Savo Island in August. (US Naval Historical Center)

THE BATTLE OF SAVO ISLAND

This series of views is from the deck of the cruiser *Aoba* during the Battle of Savo Island. The Japanese ship has illuminated the American cruiser *Quincy*. In the first frame, the American cruiser is visible by the glare of searchlights at 9,200 yards. In the second frame, *Aoba* has fired at the target and splashes are evident around the American ship, which still has her turrets trained fore and aft. In the third frame, the American ship is hit by 8-inch shells. In the final frame, the *Quincy* is hit by a torpedo that seals her fate.

Despite being riddled with shells and set afire, *Quincy* bravely fought back. One of her salvos scored the most serious blow suffered by the Japanese in the battle, when two or three shells hit the bridge of Mikawa's flagship *Chokai*, landing a mere 20 ft from where the Japanese admiral was standing, killing or wounding 36 men. *Quincy* finally succumbed after taking three torpedoes and innumerable hits from Japanese shells. She rolled over and sank at 0238 hours, becoming the first ship to litter the bottom of soon what would be called Iron Bottom Sound.

Picket Ships	Destroyers *Blue, Ralph Talbot*
Southern Group	Heavy cruisers *Australia, Canberra, Chicago*
	Destroyers *Bagley, Patterson*
Northern Group	Heavy cruisers *Astoria, Quincy, Vincennes*
	Destroyers *Helm, Wilson*
Eastern Group	Light cruisers *San Juan, Hobart* (Australian)
	Destroyers *Monssen, Buchanan*

The total Allied force of six heavy cruisers, two light cruisers, and eight destroyers possessed a greater combat strength than their Japanese opponents. However the deployment of the Allied force was faulty; it was too dispersed and therefore liable to defeat in detail. The flawed deployment was compounded by command difficulties. On the night of the August 8 Crutchley took *Australia* out of position for a conference with Turner, leaving the captain of *Chicago* in charge of the Southern Group. When the conference was over he did not return to the Southern Group, but patrolled north of the beachhead. He neglected to tell the commanders of the other groups any of this.

The key element of the battle was the total surprise gained by the Japanese force. Earlier, on August 8, Allied search planes had spotted Mikawa's force heading south. The reports from these aircraft were either delayed or inaccurate, or both. What reached Turner was a report that three cruisers, three destroyers, and two seaplane tenders were active well north of Guadalcanal. From this Turner assumed that the Japanese were establishing a seaplane base, not rushing south for a night engagement against superior forces. The Americans missed other opportunities to avoid total surprise. Early on the morning of August 9, as the Japanese neared the area, they steered undetected between the two radar-equipped American destroyers as related from the bridge of *Chokai*:

Astoria pictured on August 6, 1942 prior to the landings on Tulagi and Guadalcanal. Within days the ship would be sunk. (US Naval Historical Center)

At 2240 [August 8] the unmistakable form of Savo Island appeared twenty degrees on the port bow, and the tension of approaching action was set three minutes later when a lookout shouted, "Ship approaching [the *Blue*], thirty degrees starboard!"... It was a destroyer, at ten thousand meters, about to cross our bows from right to left.

An order was radioed: "Stand by for action!"

... with no change in speed she made a starboard turn and proceeded in the direction she had come, totally unaware of our approach.

The second patrolling destroyer, *Ralph Talbot,* also failed to detect the onrushing Japanese force. Once again Japanese vision would prove superior to American electronics. Not even the presence of floatplanes launched from the Japanese cruisers about an hour later could alert the Americans. The stage was set for the greatest Japanese surface combat victory of the war.

During the afternoon of the previous day, Mikawa had signaled his battle plan to his force of eight ships:

We will penetrate south of Savo Island and torpedo the enemy main force at Guadalcanal. Thence we will move toward the forward area at Tulagi and strike with torpedoes and gunfire, after which we will withdraw to the north of Savo Island.

This simple plan was essentially how the battle unfolded. Mikawa deployed his ships in a simple line-ahead formation with 1,300 yards between ships allowing free use of guns and torpedoes. Each of the cruisers hoisted a large 23-foot-long white streamer as an identification aid.

Once again Japanese lookouts provided the first warning when at 0136 hours on August 9, *Chokai* spotted the ships of the Southern Group. The Japanese opened the action with *Chokai* firing four torpedoes at *Canberra*; all missed. Simultaneously *Chokai*'s lookouts spotted the Northern Group at an incredible 18,000 yards. Minutes later lookouts on the destroyer *Patterson* finally spotted the Japanese cruisers. As she issued a warning, Japanese floatplanes did their job by illuminating the ships of the Southern Group with flares. This was the sign for the Japanese to open their attack in earnest. *Canberra* was the first ship to receive the attentions of Mikawa's cruisers. The Australian vessel was able to dodge the torpedoes fired at her, but the opening salvos of 8-inch gunfire from *Chokai* at just 4,500 yards proved devastating. Hits were scored on the bridge, killing the ship's captain, and in her engineering spaces, bringing the ship to a halt. Three more cruisers directed their 8-inch shellfire at *Canberra*; in total 24 hits were recorded, setting the ship on fire. This ultimately was enough to cause her destruction; another seven torpedoes fired at her by *Aoba* and *Furutaka* all missed. *Patterson* engaged the Japanese with gunfire, but was also quickly struck and damaged by their shells. The destroyer withdrew to the southeast. The destroyer *Bagley* launched an ineffectual torpedo attack and disappeared to the northeast.

The cruiser *Chicago* was the last ship of the Southern Group to come into contact with the Japanese. The first hint for her captain that she was under attack was a report of several nearby torpedo tracks. One torpedo scored a glancing blow on her bow, and

OVERLEAF
At the height of the Battle of Savo Island Japanese 8-inch shells and torpedoes have heavily damaged American cruisers *Quincy*, *Astoria*, and *Vincennes*. All are on fire and will eventually sink.

HMAS *Canberra* shown still burning the morning after the Battle of Savo Island. Destroyers *Blue* and *Patterson* are standing by to rescue survivors. The cruiser was later scuttled. (US Naval Historical Center)

a second scored a direct hit aft in the area of the engine rooms but did not explode. *Chicago* attempted to support *Patterson*, but succeeded only in taking herself out of the battle and leaving the transports exposed. None of the ships of the Southern Group bothered to make a proper report to the other groups; the effect was that the remainder of the Allied force remained oblivious to the scale of the Japanese attack.

After dealing with the Southern Group in just minutes, Mikawa decided to head to the northeast to attack the group of ships previously sighted. The skipper of the cruiser *Vincennes* was the commander of the Northern Group. He remained unaware of the size and location of Mikawa's approaching cruiser force. At 0150 hours the battle came to a climax when Mikawa fell upon the cruisers of the Northern Force. Using their searchlights, the Japanese cruisers quickly found their targets. *Chokai* illuminated *Astoria* at 7,700 yards; *Aoba* found *Quincy* at 9,200 yards and *Kako* spotlighted *Vincennes* at 10,500 yards. Surprise was total and the effect of Japanese gunfire devastating, as reflected in this account:

> The initial firing range of seven thousand meters closed with amazing swiftness. Every salvo caused another enemy ship to burst into flames
> For incredible minutes the turrets of enemy ships remained in their trained-in, secured positions, and we stood amazed. Yet thankful while they did not bear on us. Strings of machine-gun tracers wafted back and forth between the enemy and ourselves, but such minor counterefforts merely made a colorful spectacle, and gave us no concern. Second by second, however, the range decreased. And now we could actually distinguish the shapes of individuals running along the decks of enemy ships. The fight was getting to close quarters.

Japanese gunnery quickly found their marks. *Aoba* and *Kako* scored hits on their third salvo and *Chokai* on her fifth.

Quincy suffered the worst. Early salvos from *Aoba* created a fire fed by the *Quincy's* floatplanes and also hit the American cruiser's bridge. Before she was able to fire a single round, three Japanese cruisers, *Aoba, Furutaka,* and *Tenryu,* were pouring fire into her. She bravely headed directly for the Japanese but could get off only three salvos before being pounded out of action. The ship's assistant gunnery officer reported the condition on the ship's bridge:

> When I reached the bridge level I found it a shambles of dead bodies with only three or four people still standing. In the Pilot House itself the only person standing was the signalman at the wheel who was vainly endeavoring to check the ship's swing to starboard to bring her to port. On questioning him I found out that the Captain, who at that time was laying [*sic*] near the wheel, had instructed him to beach the ship and he was trying to head for Savo Island, distant some four miles on the port quarter. I stepped to the port side of the Pilot House, and looked out to find the island and noted that the ship was heeling rapidly to port, sinking by the bow.

A view taken from a Japanese cruiser during the Battle of Savo Island showing *Quincy* illuminated by searchlights. (US Naval Historical Center)

Aoba and *Tenryu* had scored a total of three torpedo hits; combined with 54 shell hits of various sizes this was enough guarantee *Quincy*'s destruction and the loss of 370 of her crew. In return, *Quincy* had inflicted the only significant damage of the battle on the Japanese when she landed two 8-inch rounds in the chartroom of Mikawa's flagship *Chokai*, barely missing the admiral and his staff.

Under fire from *Kako*, *Vincennes* was able to retaliate with an 8-inch salvo that damaged *Kinugasa*. *Kako* quickly began to score hits amidships, which created a fire, again fed by the American cruiser's floatplanes. Two torpedoes from *Chokai* hit the cruiser early in the battle and a third torpedo hit was later scored by *Yubari*. As many as 74 shells struck the cruiser. She sank with the loss of 332 crewmen.

The reaction by *Astoria* to the sudden Japanese attack reflected the confusion throughout the Northern Force. The ship's gunnery officer quickly ordered his 8-inch guns to fire after he observed the first few salvos from *Chokai*, but when the ship's skipper arrived on the bridge he quickly countermanded his subordinate:

> Who sounded the general alarm? Who gave the order to commence firing? I think we are firing on our own ships. Let's not get excited and act too hasty. Cease firing.

Chokai scored hits on two of *Astoria*'s three 8-inch turrets, but *Astoria* was able to fire 53 8-inch rounds before her last turret was silenced. Gunfire from *Aoba*, *Kinugasa*, and *Kako* finished off the cruiser by placing between 34 and 63 8-inch rounds into the cruiser. She sank with 216 of her crew.

The last action of the night was just after 0200 hours when the Japanese force came upon the destroyer *Ralph Talbot* still on patrol north of Savo Island. In a short action the Japanese light cruisers shattered the destroyer with 5.5-inch gunfire before the American ship could escape into a rain squall. With this the Battle of Savo Island was over.

Mikawa had scored a great victory. With minimal damage he had taken on and destroyed two groups of Allied cruisers. Little stood between him and the American invasion fleet, composed of five transports off Tulagi guarded by two destroyers and three destroyer transports, and the bulk of the transport fleet off Guadalcanal, with 13 transports escorted by another three destroyers and five old destroyer minesweepers. Following his neutralization of the Southern Force, Mikawa had an open path to the transport fleet off Lunga Point. His decision to turn north and engage the Northern Force reflected his, and the Imperial Navy's, concept of sea control. It was more important to destroy the enemy's warships than to concentrate on transports. Once the enemy's fleet had been defeated, sea control, and ultimately control of the island, would pass to the Japanese. By the time Mikawa had dealt with the Northern Force, it was past 0200 hours and his force was scattered into several sections. By his calculation, it would take several hours to reform his force before he could move to attack the transport fleet. By this time it would be light and he would be exposed to air attack from the American carriers he assumed to be nearby. He could not know that Fletcher had decided to withdraw his precious carriers. Content in his knowledge that he had scored a major victory, Mikawa ordered his force to return to Rabaul. He did not know it, but he had just sacrificed the Imperial Navy's best chance of scoring a strategic victory against the US Navy off Guadalcanal and of expelling the Americans from the island.

THE BATTLE OF CAPE ESPERANCE

The next cruiser clash would wait until October. In August the Japanese had made a major, but unsuccessful, attempt to reinforce the island. They were now forced to resort to a series of high-speed runs by destroyers (the so-called Tokyo Express) to deliver troops and supplies to the island. While the Americans ruled the waters around the island by day because of their possession of the airfield, the Imperial Navy ruled the night. On October 13 an American convoy carrying the 164th Infantry Regiment of the America Division arrived off Lunga Point. With it was an American task force under Rear Admiral Norman Scott with the mission of asserting the US Navy's presence in the waters off Guadalcanal. Scott had the mission of protecting the convoy, as well as preventing Japanese attempts to reinforce the island or conduct a night bombardment of the airfield. To accomplish this, Scott had a force of:

Heavy cruisers	*Salt Lake City, San Francisco*
Light cruisers	*Boise, Helena*
Destroyers	*Buchanan, Duncan, Farenholt, Laffey, McCalla*

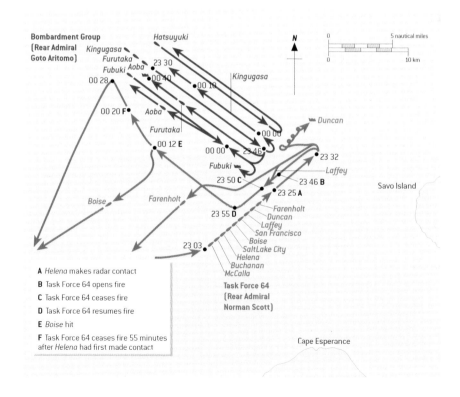

A *Helena* makes radar contact
B Task Force 64 opens fire
C Task Force 64 ceases fire
D Task Force 64 resumes fire
E *Boise* hit
F Task Force 64 ceases fire 55 minutes after *Helena* had first made contact

A pre-war (1940) view of *Helena* taken in Boston Harbor. Note the twin 5-inch/38 turrets that distinguish her from ships of the earlier *Brooklyn* class, which were fitted with 5-inch/25 single gun mounts. (US Naval Historical Center)

Scott was fully aware of the superior night-fighting techniques of the Japanese and took great pains to absorb the lessons of Savo Island. However he was still handicapped by several factors. Since the start of the war the US Navy had faced constant turnover and losses, making it unusual for any group of ships to be allowed to train and gel as a unit. Scott's force was another scratch formation of the US Navy's remaining strength in the south Pacific. Scott, and the rest of the Navy, remained ignorant of the true capabilities of the Type 93 torpedo, which negated the American preference to engage in a gunfire duel beyond the perceived range of Japanese torpedoes. Finally, the great leveling factor in a night action – American radar – was still not understood by US naval officers. The early radar, the SC type, was in service at the start of the war, but possessed only limited performance. A US Navy Fleet Bulletin from March 1942 put its effective range at 4–10 miles. This could be further degraded by the proximity of land. As Savo Island had demonstrated, possession of SC radar was no guarantee of first detection. The follow-on to the SC was the SG radar, using a narrow centimetric-wave beam rather than the SC's metric-wave beam; this gave the SG radar much superior performance but, because of the excessive secrecy surrounding its introduction, Scott was ignorant of its greater capabilities. During the upcoming battle, this difference in radar performance was important, as Scott's heavy cruisers carried the SC while his two light cruisers carried the SG. Unfortunately Scott chose the traditional method of using a heavy cruiser as his flagship.

Scott's plan for his task force was simple and, more importantly, executable by his makeshift command. He would deploy his ships in a column with destroyers deployed ahead and astern of the four cruisers. The destroyers were ordered to illuminate targets with their searchlights after they had gained radar contact. They were to use their torpedoes against big targets and engage smaller targets with their 5-inch guns. The cruisers would no longer have to wait for orders to fire; they were ordered to open fire as soon as they had a target. Cruiser floatplanes would be used to illuminate targets, like the Japanese had done at Savo. Scott was aware of the Japanese torpedo threat, and planned to divide his force into smaller sections if the threat was judged to be significant. Perhaps most important of all, Scott had the opportunity to use these tactics in some pre-battle exercises with his force.

The Japanese were also planning to reinforce their Guadalcanal garrison, and the night run on October 11 was slated to include two high-speed seaplane carriers bearing artillery. Accompanying the seaplane tenders were six destroyers, five of which had their decks full of troops.

In addition to the transport operation the Imperial Navy planned to execute the first large-scale bombardment of Henderson Field with surface ships. The bombardment would be conducted at night and would use shells fused to cause maximum damage to the aircraft at the field. The Japanese assumed no US Navy ships would challenge their night dominance of the waters around Guadalcanal. The ships assigned the mission under the command of Rear Admiral Goto Aritomo, commander of Cruiser Division 6, included:

Heavy cruisers	*Aoba, Furutaka, Kinugasa*
Destroyers	*Fubuki, Hatsuyuki*

Scott had conducted sweeps into the waters north of Guadalcanal on October 9 and 10 with no contact. The next night the Imperial Navy was present and the second major battle on the waters north of the island was on. Scott led his force to a point northwest of Guadalcanal and to the west of Savo Island where he set up a northeasterly–southwesterly patrol line. Unlike at Savo Island, American radar came into play early in the battle. At 2325 hours, the SG radar aboard *Helena* picked up a contact at 27,700 yards. However the ship's captain did not report this to Scott. About the time of the radar detection by *Helena*, Scott's force was nearing the northernmost part of its patrol line. At 2332 Scott ordered his force to reverse course. Instead of the entire column pivoting on a single point and maintaining formation, some of the cruisers executed an immediate turn, placing the forward destroyers on their starboard flank and throwing the column into disarray. This was to have serious consequences in the upcoming minutes. As the three van destroyers were racing down the starboard side of the cruiser column to regain their place in the front of Scott's formation, the battle broke out.

Scott's pre-battle plans called for the cruiser captains to open fire at their own discretion. *Helena* had been tracking the Japanese since 2325 but, presumably because of the confusion regarding the location of the van destroyers, did not open fire. By

2345, the range had closed to a mere 3,600 yards and the Japanese were visible to American lookouts. Still unclear of his destroyers' location and fearful of firing upon them, Scott, aboard *San Francisco* without the benefit of SG radar, never did give permission to engage. At 2346 after a confused radio exchange with Scott, the captain of the *Helena* finally opened fire on his own initiative.

However, the confused American approach to battle was nothing compared to the inertia and unpreparedness on the Japanese side. Goto's mission demanded a high-speed approach and exit to the target area so he could be far from the island by dawn to avoid possible air attack. As has already been mentioned, the Japanese admiral shared the Imperial Navy's general conviction that no American force would challenge him in a night battle. Accordingly, he and his force were totally unprepared, an oversight that would cost Goto his life and hand the Japanese their first defeat in a night engagement. Because he expected no opposition, the report at 2343 by Japanese lookouts of three ships at 10,000 meters, prompted Goto to flash a query to what he assumed were friendly ships. His lookouts quickly identified the contacts as American ships, but Goto still failed to act.

After the mutual series of errors and delays, the tactical situation at the onset of battle favored the Americans. Scott's patrol line placed him in a position of "capping the T" of the Japanese force. In the words of the captain of *Salt Lake City*, "It was one of those things that naval officers wait twenty years to see. We crossed their T." The leading ship in Goto's formation was the cruiser *Aoba* and it was Goto's flagship that took an early beating from gunfire from *Boise*, *Salt Lake City*, and two destroyers. *Aoba* suffered crippling damage that knocked out her two forward 8-inch turrets, destroyed her main battery fire control, and killed Goto on his bridge. In response to

THE BATTLE OF CAPE ESPERANCE

Looking from the bridge of USS *Helena* during the Battle of Cape Esperance, the Japanese force has closed to within some 3,600 yards. At this range, the ships are now visible to the naked eye. Lookouts about the American cruiser are able to make out three heavy cruisers and a destroyer.

the deluge of American fire, *Aoba*, *Furutaka*, and a destroyer made a turn to starboard; *Kinugasa* and *Hatsuyuki* made a turn to port and thus escaped most of the devastation that followed.

Since Scott had never issued orders to fire, he quickly ordered a ceasefire at 2347 that only the two heavy cruisers adhered to. Still convinced he was firing on his own destroyers, Scott delayed permission to reopen fire until 2351 after he was satisfied that the targets were Japanese. But, in fact, Scott had reason to be concerned. He already suspected that three of his destroyers were between the two opposing cruiser forces; he did not know that one of these, *Duncan*, was already under fire from both sides. When *Duncan* made her turn before the start of the battle to assume a southwesterly course, she made radar contact on the Japanese four miles away and immediately changed course to close on the contact. Just before the start of the battle, one of her crewmen described her situation:

> One moment I saw nothing but darkness and the faint sheen of starlight on calm seas. The next moment, ghostly forms took shape. Ships seemed to suddenly leap out of the darkness … I called out: "Enemy ships – visible to the naked eye!"

Completed in September 1939, *Helena* had a brief but very eventful career. Damaged at Pearl Harbor, she returned in time to participate in the Battle of Cape Esperance. Later, she survived the vicious night battle off Guadalcanal on November 13, 1942. She was sunk in July 1943 by Japanese destroyers in the Battle of Kula Gulf. She is shown here in 1943; wartime censors have deleted her radar. (US Naval Historical Center)

When the battle opened, *Duncan* was engaged by the Japanese only 1,000 yards away and by radar-directed 6-inch gunfire from *Helena*. In response, she missed *Furutaka* with torpedoes but did score 5-inch hits on the cruiser before she was set ablaze. The crew abandoned ship and the destroyer sank the next day. *Farenholt* was also the victim of 6-inch gunfire and was forced to retire from the battle. *Laffey* was undamaged before she assumed a position in the rear of the American column.

As the Japanese force broke into two sections and headed northwesterly, they were able to mount a feeble response to the barrage of American shells. *Aoba's* early response amounted to seven rounds from her undamaged aft 8-inch turret. *Furutaka* managed a salvo from her secondary 4.7-inch battery and later sent 30 8-inch shells towards her tormenters. In return she became the target of concerted American shelling, which wrecked her aft 8-inch turret and set her port torpedoes on fire. Shells also hit two of her engine rooms, but she maintained her northwesterly course. Also during this period, the destroyer *Fubuki* came under heavy fire. In minutes she exploded and sank.

The second phase of the battle began at 2353 when Scott turned his force to the northwest in pursuit of the fleeing Japanese. He still retained control of his four cruisers and the destroyers *Buchanan* and *McCalla*. At this point the damaged *Aoba* and *Furutaka* were subject to heavy shelling. Both ships suffered severe damage, with *Furutaka* taking more than 90 hits and *Aoba* more than 40. Damage to *Furutaka* eventually brought her to a halt and flooding sank her later that morning. Despite her damage *Aoba* was able to depart the area and lived to fight again. The only effective response by the Imperial Navy was made by *Kinugasa*. Her turn to port early in the battle took her out of the first phase of combat. Now, at about midnight, she reentered the battle, first engaging *San Francisco* with gunfire and then launching torpedoes at *Boise*. When *Boise* employed her searchlights, *Kinugasa* engaged her with 8-inch gunfire and quickly scored a hit on her forward barbette. This was followed by an 8-inch hit on *Boise's* hull below the waterline that entered the ship's forward magazine and started a fierce fire. Before the war the Japanese had devoted much study to developing "diving shells" with the characteristics to score just this kind of hit. During the entire war, this was the only instance where the diving shells performed as expected. Only flooding caused by the effect of the shell, combined with the efforts of the *Boise's* crew to flood the magazine, saved the ship from destruction. *Kinugasa's* accurate gunners next scored at least two hits on *Salt Lake City*; one pierced her weak armor belt but caused only minor flooding while the second caused a major fire and resulted in loss of steering. In exchange, *Kinugasa* suffered four hits but only minor damage.

Scott terminated the pursuit of the shattered Japanese force at 0028. The Battle of Cape Esperance was over. During the battle, the Japanese Reinforcement Group continued on its mission undisturbed.

STATISTICS AND ANALYSIS

Savo Island was the worst US Navy defeat ever suffered at sea.

Four heavy cruisers were lost (one Australian), and a fifth damaged. Two destroyers were also damaged. Personnel losses were also heavy, with 1,077 sailors killed and 700 wounded.

In return, Mikawa's losses were light. *Chokai* suffered three hits that killed 34 and wounded 48. *Aoba* suffered extensive topside damage but was able to withdraw at high speed. *Kinugasa* had one killed and one wounded from two hits. *Tenryu* took a single 5-inch hit and had 23 killed and 21 wounded. The largest loss to the Japanese was suffered after the battle on August 10 when American submarine *S-44* sank *Kako* (71 dead and 15 wounded) on her way to Kavieng.

Savo Island was the epitome of the Imperial Navy's night-fighting skills. Pre-war night-fighting doctrine had proven sound in the crucible of war. Superior night optics and highly trained lookouts provided the Japanese with first detection upon which the cruisers immediately launched torpedoes. The role of the cruiser floatplanes was key, as they designated and illuminated targets. Illumination from the cruisers was also crucial, as was the clarity with which targets were designated and engaged and the accuracy of 8-inch gunfire. Despite the central role the Imperial Navy had placed on its Type 93 super-weapon, it is important to note that at Savo Island cruiser gunfire crippled the American cruisers with torpedoes only finishing off the wounded ships.

American command and control problems and faulty deployments had as much to do with the disaster at Savo as did superior Japanese doctrine. Turner's decision to use only two destroyers to guard the western approached to Savo Island was faulty, as was the decision to deploy them so close to the cruiser forces. The patrol areas of the two

Chicago was lucky to survive Savo. She is shown here the day after the battle with damage evident to her bow. She was not as fortunate several months later during the Battle of Rennell Island. She was sunk during the battle on January 29, 1943, by six aircraft torpedoes. (US Naval Historical Center)

ships could take them as far as 20 miles apart, easily big enough for an enemy force to slip through. The Allied cruisers would have been better kept together under a single commander to react as required against an incoming threat. The potential game-changer of superior American technology in the form of radar was wasted when the best radar in the entire Allied force, the SG radar aboard the new cruiser *San Juan*, was placed in the area least likely to be engaged.

Allied command problems overshadowed the brilliance of the Japanese performance. Neither Crutchley nor Turner made an attempt to brief his force ahead of time and neither issued a battle plan. With no common doctrine to fall back on, and with a force that had never trained together, the predictable result was chaos. Crutchley's unannounced removal from the Southern Force was compounded by the fact he left nobody else clearly in charge. The choice of a commander for the Northern Force, the captain of *Vincennes*, was another decision with disastrous consequences. This officer had never met Crutchley and, as already mentioned, did not know his commander's plan or intent. In any event, as a cruiser captain he would have had his hands full with fighting his own ship, much less as the commander of a group of three cruisers.

American command problems began at the top, with the commander of the Amphibious Force, Kelly Turner. He was guilty of using his available intelligence to

attempt to discern Japanese intentions without considering Japanese capabilities. He failed to guard against the most dangerous enemy course of action, launching a night-surface attack on his dispersed invasion force. In the event, this was the exact intention of the aggressive Japanese. For the Americans, the only saving grace in the entire battle was that the Japanese had not pressed their advantage and destroyed the transport fleet. Such an action would have probably spelled the end of the hurried attempt to invade Guadalcanal and would have had a strategic impact. Destruction of the American transports would have been worth the sacrifice of Mikawa's entire force.

With the element of surprise in their favor at Savo, the well-trained crews of the Imperial Navy's heavy cruisers were unbeatable. However, when the element of surprise passed to the Americans, the Japanese were far from invincible, even at night. The outcome of the Battle of Cape Esperance was therefore quite different. Undoubtedly the battle was an American victory, but not the major success that Scott claimed in his after-action report.

Japanese losses in the battle included the sinking of *Furutaka* with 258 of her crew killed and the destruction of the destroyer *Fubuki* with about 78 killed (the remainder of her crew, 111 men, was taken prisoner). The cruiser *Aoba* suffered heavy damage, but since the integrity of her hull was not compromised, she was able to retire from

Rear Admiral Kelly Turner and Major General Alexander Vandergrift confer during the battle for Guadalcanal. Despite being responsible for the disaster at Savo Island, Turner escaped personal blame and went on to have an outstanding record for the remainder of the war. (US Naval Historical Center)

the battle with 79 dead and undergo repairs in Japan. She returned to action in January 1943. The Japanese also suffered minor damage to *Kinugasa* and *Hatsuyuki*. As the Imperial Navy was unable to place blame on Goto, his chief of staff was immediately relieved.

The Americans clearly came off better, but the cost of victory was not negligible. The destroyer *Duncan* was pummeled by both sides and sank with the cost of 48 killed and 35 wounded. *Boise* suffered severe damage with 107 killed and 29 wounded; the cruiser was lucky to survive the fight. Less severe damage to *Salt Lake City* still required six months to repair. She lost five dead and 19 wounded. Damage to the destroyer *Farenholt* (also by "friendly" fire) also required a trip to the US for repairs. Personnel losses totaled three dead and 40 wounded.

The reasons for the American victory were easy to find and bear a striking resemblance to the key factors behind the Japanese victory just weeks earlier at Savo. The main determinant was surprise. Aside from Japanese carelessness, the reason for this was American use of radar. The US Navy was still learning to incorporate this new technology into its tactics, but Cape Esperance clearly showed the potential of this key technology, which had the potential to completely upset the Japanese calculus of how night battles should be fought. The Americans could take comfort in the prowess of their gunnery, especially the fast-firing 6-inchers aboard the two light cruisers. The victory had shown that the Imperial Navy was not invincible in a night battle and Scott should be given much of the credit. His tactics, while simple, were well suited to his command. An unfortunate side effect was the temptation by subsequent

Boise shown on trials in 1938. The ship was fortunate to survive damage suffered at the Battle of Cape Esperance, but went on to give distinguished service in the Mediterranean and the Pacific. (US Naval Historical Center)

American task-force commanders to use tactics similar to Scott's with less than desirable results. But what was lost in the overall disasterous performance of Goto's force at Cape Esperance was the continued excellence of individual Japanese ships, as exhibited by the superb gunnery of *Kinugasa*. Fortunately for the Americans, the Long Lance torpedo did not make itself felt during the battle.

Cape Esperance showed that the Imperial Navy could also be guilty of a lack of battle readiness. Despite signs that an American force was in the area, when the Americans opened fire not one Japanese ship was ready for action. This was solely due to Goto's irresponsibility in assuming no American challenge was possible. Even after his lookouts identified their contacts as American, Goto refused to shake his inertia. The only saving grace for the Imperial Navy was the performance of *Kinugasa*

	Cruisers sunk	Destroyers sunk	Personnel killed or captured
US	4 (1 Australian)	1	1,240
IJN	1	1	584

Damage to the Number 3 turret of *Boise* suffered during the Battle of Cape Esperance. This view was taken at Philadelphia Navy Yard in November 1942 as *Boise* began repairs from the damage suffered in the battle. (US Naval Historical Center)

and the fact that it did successfully conduct the reinforcement portion of the battle.

After the first two major surface battles of the Guadalcanal campaign, losses for each side were as shown on the table on p73.

While it is always precarious to draw conclusions from two battles so shaped by command difficulties and surprise, several trends were evident. The pre-war Japanese energy spent on developing night-combat tactics and equipment proved well spent in the early part of the Guadalcanal campaign. In general, Japanese cruiser doctrine and weaponry, and their night-fighting skill, proved superior during the first part of Pacific War. The Japanese decision to retain torpedoes aboard their cruisers was proven correct. Another crucial element of the early Japanese successes was the better-trained crews of their cruisers and destroyers.

Nevertheless, even if Japanese night-fighting skills were greater, this conferred the Imperial Navy with only a tactical edge and did not translate to decisive victory. The Japanese emphasis on quality was appropriate for a short, decisive war, but the six-month struggle for Guadalcanal showed that the Japanese were facing a protracted battle of attrition that they could not win. The US Navy made up for its lack of night-fighting skills with a collective instilled sense of aggression. This ensured that unless the Japanese fought a perfect battle, such as at Savo Island, every clash would exact a toll from the Japanese ensuring the eventual demise of the Imperial Navy. Increasingly, the successful integration of technology overcame the Japanese night-fighting skills and by late 1943 the US Navy could claim superiority in this area.

When comparing the designs of the cruisers themselves, the Imperial Navy consistently demonstrated that it could produce superior ships. This superiority began with the *Furutaka* class and lasted up until 1943 when the US Navy introduced the *Baltimore* class. The epitome of Imperial Navy cruiser design was the *Takao* class. Japanese cruisers gained a reputation as tough opponents in the early part of the war, which they maintained throughout the conflict. However their designs, even with the extra margins provided by exceeding treaty limitations, did have shortcomings. They possessed much less range and were noted for stability problems. Their increased weight also made them vulnerable to battle damage as most of their main belts were submerged.

As the war progressed, the true weakness of the Imperial Navy's cruisers was exposed. Increasingly Japanese cruisers were vulnerable to air attack. Despite a growing number of antiaircraft weapons fitted throughout the war, of the 16 heavy cruisers sunk during the war, ten were lost solely or primarily to air attack. In comparison, only two were sunk by US or Royal Navy surface forces and another four by submarine attack.

US Navy Treaty cruisers proved supremely versatile ships. While not truly outstanding in any one single capacity, they proved successful in every role they were assigned, including surface combat, carrier escort, and shore bombardment. Despite concerns about their ability to absorb damage, many Treaty cruisers survived fearful damage from Japanese torpedoes and the majority survived the war. During the Guadalcanal campaign, they ultimately proved up to the challenge and played an important part in the American victory.

AFTERMATH

When the Battle of Cape Esperance ended, the campaign for Guadalcanal was far from over. In fact the largest and fiercest battles of the six-month campaign were yet to be fought. However these battles would be different from the predominantly cruiser-on-cruiser duels of Savo and Cape Esperance.

Cruisers of both sides would continue to be very active in the waters around Guadalcanal. After a devastating bombardment of Henderson Field by two Imperial Navy battleships on October 14, *Chokai* and *Kinugasa* conducted a follow-up bombardment the next night. *Myoko* and *Maya* conducted yet another assault on the airfield on October 16.

November saw the battle for Guadalcanal come to a climax. Another Japanese attempt to conduct a battleship bombardment forced the US Navy to again engage in night combat. Against two Japanese battleships escorted by light cruisers and destroyers, the Americans committed a force including the cruisers *San Francisco, Portland, Helena*, and two *Atlanta*-class light anti-aircraft cruisers. In probably the most intense night battle of the war, the Japanese bombardment force was stopped, but the two light cruisers (*Atlanta* and *Juneau*) were sunk, and all the other cruisers damaged. The next night, on November 14, the Japanese heavy cruisers *Maya* and *Suzuya* conducted another bombardment of Henderson. *Kinugasa* was sunk by air attack the next day as she provided cover for the retiring bombardment force.

On October 14 another Japanese battleship, escorted by cruisers *Atago* and *Takao*, attempted to put Henderson out of action. This time they were met by the US Navy's most modern surface units, the battleships *Washington* and *South Dakota*. In another fierce night action the Japanese cruisers shot well, scoring many hits on *South Dakota*, but for once the Type 93 torpedo let the Japanese down. Despite many shots at short range and with good angles, no Japanese torpedo hits were scored on the US battleships, which succeeded in destroying the Japanese battleship and thwarting the Japanese operation.

The height of Japanese night-fighting prowess was at the Battle of Tassafaronga on November 30. Here eight Japanese destroyers conducting a transport mission to Guadalcanal gave the best demonstration to date of the capabilities of the Type 93 torpedo when they sank the cruiser *Northampton* and torpedoed and heavily damaged the cruisers *Minneapolis, New Orleans,* and *Pensacola.*

The sinking of *Northampton* was the fifth and last Treaty cruiser lost during the battles around Guadalcanal. For the remainder of the war only three more US Navy Treaty cruisers were lost: *Chicago* to air attack in January 1943, *Helena* to Type 93s in July 1943, and *Indianapolis* to submarine attack in 1945. For the entire war, seven of the 18 heavy Treaty cruisers were sunk and only one of the *Brooklyn* or *St. Louis* class was sunk.

None of the Imperial Navy's heavy cruisers survived the war intact. The battles around Guadalcanal saw the near annihilation of the *Furutaka* and *Aoba* classes, with three of the four ships being sunk. The only surviving unit, *Aoba,* was sunk in Japanese home waters by carrier air attack in July 1945.

The cruisers of the *Myoko* class proved to be tough and resilient opponents and all four ships of the class survived late into the war. *Myoko* herself was damaged at the Battle of Leyte Gulf and surrendered in a damaged condition in Singapore at war's end. The first to be sunk was *Nachi* when she was lost to carrier air attack in November

After an eventful wartime career, *Myoko* was surrendered at Singapore in 1945, one of only two Imperial Navy cruisers to survive the war. *Myoko* is shown here in a damaged condition with an unusual camouflage scheme. She was finally scuttled by the British in July, 1946. (Yamato Museum)

1944. *Ashigara* and *Haguro* both survived until 1945 when they were sunk by British submarine and surface forces respectively.

The powerful units of the *Takao* class were all destroyed or damaged within the span of a few days during the Battle of Leyte Gulf. US submarines torpedoed and sank *Atago* and *Maya* on October 23 and the same attack sent the damaged *Takao* to Singapore where she was surrendered at the end of the war. Two days later *Chokai* was sunk by carrier air attack.

The ships of the *Mogami* class also proved tough to sink. *Mikuma* was the first Japanese heavy cruiser lost when she was bombed during the Battle of Midway. The remainder of the class survived until 1944 when all were committed to the Imperial Navy's supreme effort at Leyte Gulf. *Mogami* was sunk by a combination of air and surface attacks after absorbing incredible damage, and *Suzuya* was sunk by air attack. *Kumano* was damaged during the battle but not finally sunk until November, when she was discovered and sunk by air attack. By war's end, of the 18 Imperial Navy heavy cruisers in commission at the start of the war, only two remained afloat, and both of these were non-operational.

Aoba pictured in Kure, Japan after the war. After serving throughout the south Pacific battles, *Aoba* was damaged by submarine attack during the Battle of Leyte Gulf. After returning to Japan, she was not repaired and was later sunk in shallow waters by carrier air attack. (US Naval Historical Center)

BIBLIOGRAPHY

The single most authoritative source on Imperial Navy cruisers in English is the magisterial *Japanese Cruisers of the Pacific War*. It is very pricey but worth every penny to the reader with a serious interest in the subject. Its counterpart for American cruisers does not exist, but Norman Friedman's *US Cruisers* comes the closest. For the single best account of the battle for Guadalcanal, including extensive and insightful accounts of the naval actions, readers are referred to Richard Frank's *Guadalcanal*.

Backer, Steve, *Japanese Heavy Cruisers*, Chatham Publishing, London (2006)

Campbell, John, *Naval Weapons of World War Two*, Naval Institute Press, Annapolis, Maryland (1985)

Cook, Charles, *The Battle of Cape Esperance*, Naval Institute Press, Annapolis, Maryland (1992)

Evans, David C. (ed.), *The Japanese Navy in World War II*, Naval Institute Press, Annapolis, Maryland (1986)

Evans, David C. and Peattie, Mark R., *Kaigun*, Naval Institute Press, Annapolis, Maryland (1997)

Frank, Richard B, *Guadalcanal*, Random House, New York (1990)

Friedman, Norman, *US Cruisers*, Naval Institute Press, Annapolis, Maryland (1984)

Hone, Thomas C. and Hone, Trent, *Battle Line*, Naval Institute Press, Annapolis, Maryland (2006)

Lacroix, Eric and Wells II, Linton, *Japanese Cruisers of the Pacific War*, Naval Institute Press, Annapolis, Maryland (1997)

Loxton, Bruce with Chris Coulthard-Clark, *The Shame of Savo*, Naval Institute Press, Annapolis, Maryland (1994)

Marriot, Leo, *Treaty Cruisers*, Pen and Sword Maritime, Barnsley (2005)

Morison, Samuel Eliot, *The Struggle for Guadalcanal*, Little, Brown and Company, Boston (1975)

O'Hara, Vincent P., *The US Navy Against the Axis*, Naval Institute Press, Annapolis, Maryland (2006)

Silverstone, Paul H., *The Navy of World War II 1922–1947*, Routledge, New York (2008)

Skulski, Janusz, *The Heavy Cruiser Takao*, Naval Institute Press, Annapolis, Maryland (1994)

Warner, Denis and Warner, Peggy with Sadao Senoo, *Disaster in the Pacific*, Naval Institute Press, Annapolis, Maryland (1992)

Watts, Anthony J. and Gordon, Brian G., *The Imperial Japanese Navy*, Macdonald, London (1971)

Whitley, M.J., *Cruisers of World War Two*, Naval Institute Press, Annapolis, Maryland (1995)

Wiper, Steve, *New Orleans Class Cruisers,* Classic Warships Publishing, Tucson, Arizona (2000)

Wiper, Steve, *Indianapolis & Portland,* Classic Warships Publishing, Tucson, Arizona (n.d.)

Indianapolis pictured in September 1939. Though slightly longer and completed with eight (vice four) 5-inch guns, the two ships of the *Indianapolis* were very similar to the preceding *Northampton* class. *Indianapolis* spent much of her service as a flagship, for which she was designed. She was the last major US Navy warship lost during the war, being sunk by submarine attack on July 30, 1945. (US Naval Historical Center)

INDEX

Figures in **bold** refer to illustrations.